UNDERSTANDING THE KINGDOM OF GOD

Also by this author:

Building Your House on the Rock

UNDERSTANDING THE KINGDOM OF GOD

IAN WILKINSON

Library of Congress Control Number:		2008908730
ISBN:	Hardcover	978-1-4363-7402-6
	Softcover	978-1-4363-7401-9

This book was printed in the United States of America.

To order additional copies of this book, contact:
Xlibris Corporation
1-888-795-4274
www.Xlibris.com
Orders@Xlibris.com
51041

~ CONTENTS ~

~ FOREWORD ~

I first came to know Ian Wilkinson when my church was hosting unity meetings with three other churches in our area. Through those meetings, a mentorship began as I attended Ian's classes on the kingdom of God. I found his teaching style dynamic and his message inspired.

I believe God has called and anointed Ian to be a teacher in the biblical standard of Ephesians 4:11. His understanding of the kingdom of God and how it affects a Christian life has brought freedom to many areas of my life. My first revelation was how water baptism, in a kingdom context, has to do with entering the kingdom of God. It is the first outward sign of obedience or evidence of faith. It is one thing to be told you have been saved from the consequences of sin in your life. It is quite another to understand how you have been set free from sinning and know how to apply that knowledge to remain free.

This book deals with the authority of the kingdom of God in our lives. Whether you are a new Christian or a seasoned warrior, there is fresh revelation for you in this book.

I believe this book is of paramount importance for all new Christians to read and understand. It is a foundational teaching that is necessary in building a strong Christian life.

—Kevin J. Taylor

~ PREFACE ~

If you want to understand the kingdom of God and be fruitful, then this book is for you. I have been a Christian for more than twenty-seven years and didn't really understand the kingdom for most of that time. I sense I am not alone in this, for I have shared this teaching in churches in North America, Europe, and Asia and rarely found anyone who can clearly define the kingdom of God.

The secret of the kingdom of God has been given to you. (Mark 4:11)

Listen then to what the parable of the sower means: When anyone hears the message about the kingdom and does not understand it, the evil one comes and snatches away what was sown in his heart. This is the seed sown along the path . . . . But the one who received the seed [the message about the kingdom] that fell on good soil is the man who hears the word and understands it. He produces a crop, yielding a hundred, sixty or thirty times what was sown. (Matt. 13:18; 13:23, NIV)

Understanding the kingdom will revitalize your Christianity and replace any weak footings with a solid foundation. Jesus asked if you don't understand the parable of the sower then how will you understand any parable (Mark 4:13)? Since the parable of the sower centers on the message of the kingdom, it follows that if you don't grasp the meaning of the kingdom you won't understand the parable either. This book is about understanding.

> *Though it cost all you have, get understanding.* (Prov. 4:7, NIV)

I discovered the meaning of the kingdom a number of years ago when I decided to take Matthew 6:33 seriously: *"Seek ye first the kingdom of God"* (KJV). As I set out to seek the kingdom one morning, I realized that I didn't know what it was I was seeking. I had to ask the Lord what it was I was supposed to be seeking.

For six months, I researched the meaning of the kingdom and for the most part, found out that authors and scholars wrote about the kingdom as if everyone knew what it was already. I did eventually find out what the kingdom is and began to make notes, thinking I would write a book. I didn't tell anyone about this at the time. A visiting man of God prophesied to me that God wanted me to write a book, and that I had already started it. He said it would be on a subject others had written about, but that it would have a clarity of understanding to it. It has taken seven years and a few rewrites but here it is.

May the Lord impart to you understanding as you read this book.

1

~ THE KINGDOM PARADOX ~

Seeking First the Kingdom of God

But seek ye first the kingdom of God, and his righteousness; and all these things shall be added unto you. (Matt. 6:33, KJV)

Define a paradox. (Please circle the letter corresponding to the best response.)

A. Mallard mates.
B. A couple of surgeons.
C. A statement seemingly self-contradictory or absurd but, in reality, expressing a truth.
D. Two piers.

The kingdom of God was central to the ministry of Jesus. He began his ministry by preaching, *"The kingdom of God is near. Repent and believe the good news."* (Mark 1:15, NIV) The Beatitudes start and finish with reference to the kingdom. The Lord's Prayer says, *"Your kingdom come."* Eighty percent of the parables teach the kingdom. When he cast out demons, Jesus explained that it displayed the power of the kingdom. Jesus talked privately with both Nicodemus in John 3:3 and Pilate in John 19:14

about the kingdom. The disciples argued about who would be greatest in the kingdom. The thief on the cross asked Jesus to remember him when he came into his kingdom. Jesus told the disciples to preach the gospel of the kingdom (Matt. 24:14) in all the world and then the end would come. He said that we would go through much tribulation to enter the kingdom. After his resurrection, Jesus spoke for forty days with his followers about the kingdom of God (Acts 1:3). Paul continued in the pattern.

Boldly and without hindrance he preached the kingdom of God and taught about the Lord Jesus Christ. (Acts 28:31, NIV)

The Gospels are full of references to the kingdom of God. It is clearly the central theme. Unfortunately, there is a problem.

Those of us who are to represent the kingdom of God on earth don't know what it is. We are king-dumb. Somehow, this priority message in the Gospels has been obscured and lost to us.

The kingdom paradox is that the people called to represent the kingdom, and to preach the kingdom, don't know what it is.

2

~ THE KINGDOM DEFINED ~

Righteousness, Peace and Joy in the Holy Spirit

For the kingdom of God is not a matter of eating and drinking, but of righteousness, peace and joy in the Holy Spirit, because anyone who serves Christ in this way is pleasing to God and approved by men. (Rom. 14:17-18, NIV)

The kingdom of God (synonymous with the kingdom of heaven in Matthew's Gospel) is not a place. It is not heaven. It is not the church. A kingdom is realm ruled by a monarch. Ern Baxter defined the kingdom of God as the government of God. This makes sense. Matthew 6:33 is thus saying: make it a priority to be governed by God. The Lord's prayer, *"Let thy kingdom come, let thy will be done"* means, "Lord, rule in my life today."

The Kingdom of God = the Government of God

We enter the kingdom of God when we, of our own free will, submit to the Lordship of Jesus Christ. *"That if you confess with your mouth, 'Jesus is Lord,' and believe in your heart that God raised Him from the dead, you will be saved"* (Rom. 10:9). The kingdom of God is the government of God that we voluntarily surrender to. We did this when we first believed, and we can continue to do it daily.

Another definition comes from an elderly Australian lady I met when she and I were both visiting Romford, a town northeast of London, England. She defined it as the rule of Christ. *Christ* means *anointing* or *anointed*. It is a term that refers to Jesus as the Anointed or the Messiah (the Christ). It also refers to the Holy Spirit, who is the Anointing. Jesus stands, or sits, at the right hand of God the Father. He is a resurrected man. *"For there is one God, and one mediator between God and men, the man [anthropos-human] Christ Jesus"* (1 Tim. 2:5, NIV). Jesus, the man, does not live in our hearts physically. He lives there by his Spirit. So the Christ in us is the Holy Spirit.

We read in Romans 14:17 that the kingdom of God is in the Holy Spirit. The Holy Spirit is in us if we are indeed true disciples of Christ. We must allow the Spirit in us to govern us. *"You, however, are controlled not by the sinful nature but by the Spirit."* (Rom. 8:9, NIV). The kingdom of God is the rule of the Holy Spirit. Being in the kingdom means allowing the Spirit to administer our lives instead of allowing sin to control us.

The Kingdom of God = the Rule of Christ

Now Matthew 6:33 really makes sense. Seek ye first the kingdom of God means make it a priority to be governed by the Holy Spirit. Let God be in control of your life. Let Jesus truly be Lord. It's a daily surrender.

Now that we have defined the kingdom of God as the government of God, or the rule of Christ, let's look at Romans 14:17-18 again:

> For the [government of God] is not a matter of eating and drinking, but of righteousness, peace and joy in the Holy Spirit, because anyone who serves Christ in this way is pleasing to God and approved by men.

This passage is more of a description than a definition. The kingdom is not a matter of outward rules or rituals concerning what you can eat or drink. It is a matter of righteousness, peace, and joy in the Holy Spirit. It is a matter of serving Christ. The key is "serving." We serve Christ by obeying him.

The person under the government of God is not seeking to be justified. He is already justified. He is seeking to serve or please God as disciple of the Lord Jesus. So we are not serving to be justified. We are serving because we are justified. We are not trying to earn sonship but to express sonship. This is important to establish because it affects how we define righteousness.

Righteousness, Peace, and Joy in the Holy Spirit

Righteousness is both a gift and a fruit. We receive the gift of righteousness when we first confess Jesus as Lord and believe in our hearts that he is raised from the dead. This gift, coupled with abundance of grace, allows us to reign in life (Rom. 5:17). Jesus paid for this gift with his own blood on Calvary. It is by his blood, it is the work of Jesus, that makes us right before God. So faith in Jesus and his blood justifies or makes us in right standing or right being before God. Faith helps us see and enter the kingdom.

Justification is the righteousness of right standing with God and is a gift paid for by Jesus on Calvary and accepted by faith into the life of the believer.

The fruit of righteousness is right living or right doing. It is also called sanctification. Justification is when you are legally set apart for God or made sacred or holy to him. Sanctification is the process of becoming holy in our behaviour. It is the process of learning to live right or do right in God's eyes. It is the work of the Holy Spirit in us that sanctifies us. Therefore, since living under the rule of Christ is a matter of serving, it is principally concerned with the righteousness of right living. Right living springs or grows from right standing.

Sanctification is the process of learning appropriate behaviour as a child of God. It is the work of the Holy Spirit and results as we, by faith, obey him.

Right-doing means doing what is right. *Right* is defined as anything that is the will of God. The will of God is revealed in the Word of God. Righteousness (of right-doing) is simply obedience to God. It is letting Jesus be our God-Lord-Master. We submit to the Word and the Spirit.

What will happen to you if you bow your knee before God's throne? What will happen if you start to make a conscious effort to let Jesus control your life? First, I'll tell you what Jesus won't do. He won't smack you on the head with a big stick and say, "It's about time!" He will say, "Come up here and sit with me, and we will rule together."

When we make Jesus king, then he makes us kings. I think it is to the degree that we let Jesus rule our lives that he lets us rule over the circumstances of life. As we come under authority, we are given authority. So the kingdom is not just about being governed by the Spirit and the Word, but about walking in the power and victory of the Spirit over sickness, spiritual darkness, financial problems, bondages, fears, and so on. It is reigning in life. It is walking according to love.

> *For if by the one man's offense death reigned through the one, much more those who receive abundance of grace and of the gift of righteousness will reign in life through the One, Jesus Christ.* (Rom. 5:17, NKJV)

Love is fulfilling the law and obeying his commands. *"This is love for God: to obey his commands"* (1 John 5:3, NIV). *"Love is the fulfillment of the law"* (Rom. 13:10, NIV). The Greek word for love is *agape. Agape* means "a commitment to do right for another regardless of emotion." It is a commitment to do what God says to do in the Word. Both righteousness and love fulfill the will or law of God. They are related.

Agape = A commitment to do right
for another regardless of emotion.

Peace is more than the absence of anxiety. It means nothing missing, nothing broken. It means health and wholeness, prosperity and success in the things of God. Peace relates to covenant and includes all the benefits of the cross. (These are listed at the end of this chapter.)

Peace is a gift and a fruit. *"Peace I give to you,"* Jesus said (John 14:27). When we first trusted in Jesus, we were given peace with God (Rom. 5:1). There is also the peace of God (Phil. 4:6-7). Peace comes from obeying the prince of peace (Isa. 9:6-7). Peace is fruit. *"But the fruit of the Spirit is love, joy, peace."* (Gal. 5:22, NIV). The peace mentioned in Romans 14:17 is fruit. Notice the similarity between Romans 14:17 and Galatians 5:22.

Rom. 14:17 Government of God	Righteousness Doing Right	Peace	Joy
Gal. 5:22 Fruit of the Spirit	Love Commitment to do Right	Joy	Peace

Joy is a gift and a fruit as well. Joy is associated with prayer, as in John 16:24 and Isaiah 56:7: *"These will I bring to my holy mountain and give them joy in my house of prayer"* (NIV) and with witnessing as in Psalm 51:12-13 and Luke 10:17. It is most often associated with the presence of God and with strength. *"You will fill me with joy in your presence"* (Ps. 16:11, NIV). *"In thy presence is fullness of joy"* (Ps. 16:11, KJV). The joy of the Lord is our strength (Neh. 8:10). God gives us his joy so we can serve him with his strength. Joy also speaks of the benefit of simply knowing God, the beauty of having sins forgiven, and the hope we have for the future.

We cannot serve Christ in our own strength but only by his grace. God resists the proud (self-sufficient) but gives grace to the humble. Serving God is to be a joy, not a burden (Deut. 28:47-48). To serve God joyfully means we need to be constantly filled with the Holy Spirit.

Righteousness, Peace, and Joy Relate to Covenant

> *For this is the covenant that I will make with the house of Israel after those days, says the Lord: I will put My laws in their mind and write them on their hearts; and I will be their God, and they shall be My people.* (Heb. 8:10, NKJV)

As God has said: "I will live with them and walk among them, and I will be their God, and they will be my people." (2 Cor. 6:16, NIV)

I said that peace relates to covenant. Actually, all three elements—righteousness, peace, and joy—relate to covenant. God's covenant can be expressed as three statements:

I will be your God.
You will be my people.
I will be with you.

"I will be your God" means God gets to be God. He is the authority. He is the Lord. It is his laws that are written in our hearts and minds. We follow his laws, teachings, and commandments. *"You will be my people"* means we have access to all covenant blessings including salvation, peace, health, prosperity, wisdom. It speaks of the benefits of relationship and sonship. We reign in life through one man, Christ Jesus. *"I will be with you"* means the continual blessing of his presence in which there is fullness of joy. This joy is our strength.

A disciple of Jesus Christ has God's law written in his heart and in his mind. He walks under the government of God, according to the covenant that we have with God. To know how to be ruled by the Spirit, we need to know the covenant or testament—both the Old and New testaments. Disciples of the King understand that they enjoy special privilege with God and a special responsibility before God. We know God for who he really is: LORD (Heb. 8:11), and we treat him accordingly. The government of God, or the rule of Christ, expressed as righteousness, peace, and joy relates to these three aspects of covenant.

A disciple of Jesus Christ has God's law
written in his heart and in his mind.
He walks under the government of God
according to the covenant.

Covenant	Kingdom of God
I will be your God.	Obedience to God: Righteousness
You will be my people.	The benefits of being God's child: Peace
I will be with you.	The ongoing presence of God: Joy

Entering the kingdom of God is coming under Jesus's government. We submit to his Lordship and learn his ways. He initially gives us right-standing with him and then empowers us with the Spirit to produce the fruit of right-living. Through the obedience of faith, we come under his authority and learn of him. Then we can exercise authority. We can enjoy all the benefits of sonship. He promises that he will be with us always. His joy and the privilege of his intimate fellowship strengthen us.

Benefits of the Cross:

1. Jesus was punished that we might be forgiven.
2. Jesus was wounded that we might be healed. Isaiah 53:4-5 reveals that Jesus bore the consequences of our sin on both the spiritual and physical planes. Our sins are forgiven, and our sickness is healed (1 Pet. 1:24).
3. Jesus was made sin with our sinfulness that we might become righteous with his righteousness. *"For He [God] made Him [Jesus] who knew no sin* to be *sin for us, that we might become the righteousness of God in Him"* (2 Cor. 5:21, NKJV).
4. Jesus died our death that we might share his life (Rom. 6:23 and Heb. 2:9). Jesus tasted death for everyone.
5. Jesus became poor with our poverty that we might become rich with his riches. *"That you through his poverty might become rich"* (2 Cor. 8:9, NIV). While Jesus walked this earth, he was not poor. He had all that he needed to do the will of God in his own life.

On the cross, Jesus was hungry, thirsty, naked, and in need, and he had to be buried in a borrowed tomb. (See also 2 Cor. 9:8.)

6. Jesus bore our shame that we might share his glory.

7. Jesus endured rejection that we might have his acceptance as children of God. Jesus suffered rejection and shame for us (Matt 27:46). *"[Jesus] endured the cross, despising the shame* (Heb. 12:2, NKJV), *bringing many sons to glory"* (Heb. 2:10, NKJV). *"He made us accepted in the Beloved"* (Eph. 1:5-6, KJV).

8. Jesus became a curse that we might receive a blessing. *"Christ has redeemed us from the curse of the law . . . that the blessing of Abraham might come upon the Gentiles"* (Gal. 3:13-14, NKJV).

When Jesus had accomplished all this for us on the cross, he said, *"It is finished."* The blessing of Abraham comes to us. *Bless* means to empower to prosper—spiritually, socially, physically, and financially.

3

~ THE NEW BIRTH REDEFINED ~

Seeing and Entering the Kingdom

One enters the kingdom of God, or the rule of Christ, through a process called the new birth. You could say that being born again is coming under new management or being digitally remastered. Too often, we have equated being born again with "being saved" and not considered the component of government. In fact, because it's so prevalent to consider the new birth synonymous to salvation, I must diffuse any potential misunderstanding.

Salvation can mean "safe from hell." I'm glad to be safe from hell. One of the things that motivated me to explore the claims of Christ was the suspicion that hell might exist. We know that whosoever calls on the name of the Lord can be saved. If you are a sinner dying in a car accident and call on Jesus with your last remaining gasps, you can be forgiven and go to heaven. In that instance, you were saved from hell. You were saved from the consequences of your sin, but you died before you had the opportunity to grow as a child of God. Your by-the-skin-of-your-teeth escape hardly qualifies as experiencing kingdom life—righteousness, peace, and joy. You never really became a disciplined follower of Jesus.

Salvation has another meaning: "salvaged from sins." Jesus came to save us from our sins (Matt. 1:21), not just the consequences of sin. The apostles and early disciples would have understood salvation this way. They saw it as a process, salvaging us from sins, here in this life, not as fire insurance for the afterlife. We are given salvation as a free gift, but we work out that salvation in fear and trembling.

Because the "safe from hell" connotation of salvation is so strong in our thinking, I want to separate *the new birth* from salvation, for a moment, and give it a different association. I want to develop its kingdom or governmental context.

> *Now there was a man of the Pharisees named Nicodemus, a member of the Jewish ruling council. He came to Jesus at night and said, "Rabbi, we know you are a teacher who has come from God. For no one could perform the miraculous signs you are doing if God were not with him." In reply Jesus declared, "I tell you the truth, no one can see the kingdom of God unless he is born again." "How can a man be born when he is old?" Nicodemus asked. "Surely he cannot enter a second time into his mother's womb to be born!" Jesus answered, "I tell you the truth, no one can enter the kingdom of God unless he is born of water and the Spirit." (John 3:1-5, NIV)*

Jesus said, *"I tell you the truth, no one can see the kingdom of God unless he is born again."* Please note that Jesus did not say, *"I tell you the truth, no one can be saved unless he is born again."* The subject is not salvation. It is the kingdom. In fact, it is about "seeing" the kingdom. Jesus was saying no one can get a revelation of the government of God unless he is born again. We first need to see the government of God.

Then Jesus said, *"I tell you the truth, no one can enter the kingdom of God unless he is born of water and the Spirit."* Again, he is talking about the kingdom, not salvation per se. This time he is focusing on entering the kingdom. So there is a seeing and a subsequent entering the government of God. First, the kingdom is revealed, and then realized. So the new birth is about the government of God. It is about seeing and entering it.

Being born again starts when you hear the word of God preached and conviction touches your heart. *"For you have been born again, . . . through the living and enduring word of God"* (1 Pet. 1:23, NIV). Faith comes by hearing the word of God. We accept the message of the Gospel, which calls us to repent. We repent and believe in the Lord Jesus. That, simply put, is the beginning of a new life. According to Jesus, you are now at the stage where you can see the government of God, or the rule of Christ. You haven't entered it yet. You enter the rule of Christ by being born of water and the Spirit.

Jesus commissioned his followers to go and make disciples. A disciple of Christ has recognized and accepted the Lordship of Jesus. He is under new management—an apprentice. We make disciples by baptizing them and by teaching them to obey all that Jesus commanded.

> *Then Jesus came to them and said, "All authority in heaven and on earth has been given to me. Therefore go and make disciples of all nations, baptizing them in the name of the Father and of the Son and of the Holy Spirit, and teaching them to obey everything I have commanded you. And surely I am with you always, to the very end of the age."* (Matt. 28:18-20, NIV)

If a disciple is an apprentice of Jesus (submitted to his leadership, under his government), then there must be a connection between being born again and becoming a disciple. Jesus does not commission us to simply preach good news and have people make decisions, but to make disciples. Let's take a closer look at his commission.

"All authority in heaven and on earth has been given to me." This statement is a declaration of the Lordship of Jesus Christ. He is, in fact, saying I AM God. He is stating his sovereignty. Many people forget this part of the commission. This is a kingdom statement. The great commission is stated in a kingdom context. *Therefore go and make disciples of all nations.* "Therefore" alludes to the first statement. In other words, he is saying, because I am sovereign, go and tell people in all ethnic groups. Make them my disciples. Let them know me, for who I am, Lord. Make them subjects of my rule, by *baptizing them* (immersing them in water) *in the name of the Father and of the Son and of the Holy Spirit: and teaching them to obey.*

What are we to teach new believers to obey? We are to teach everything Jesus commanded us. It sounds like Jesus is under the impression that he is in charge. He is saying, Go and teach people to obey my commands. Apparently, we are supposed to get them to come under God's government.

"*And surely I am with you always, to the very end of the age,*" is the promise of his empowering presence.

Peter understood the meaning and context of Matthew 28:18-20. He stood up on the day of Pentecost and declared the Lordship of Jesus Christ. The people responded to the Gospel of the kingdom by asking what they must do. Peter instructed them as follows: Repent and be baptized, in the name of Jesus Christ, for the forgiveness of your sins. And you will receive the gift of the Holy Spirit. He told them, in effect, to be born of water and the Spirit.

> "*Therefore let all Israel be assured of this: God has made this Jesus, whom you crucified, both Lord and Christ.*" *When the people heard this, they were cut to the heart and said to Peter and the other apostles, "Brothers, what shall we do?" Peter replied, "Repent and be baptized, every one of you, in the name of Jesus Christ for the forgiveness of your sins. And you will receive the gift of the Holy Spirit.*" (Acts 2:36-38, NIV)

Jesus told Nicodemus that in order to enter the kingdom (to submit to the rule of Christ), he must be born of water and the Spirit. Water baptism was symbolic of dying to the old life and starting anew with old sins removed. Water baptism is also the first outward step of obedience that a new believer takes. In order to come under new government, one must first die to the old.

Secondly, in order to operate in the kingdom (under God's government), you need to be empowered with divine enablement. You need the Spirit spoken of in Ezekiel 36:26-27: "*I will give you a new heart and put a new spirit in you; I will remove from you your heart of stone and give you a heart of flesh. And I will put my Spirit in you and move you to follow my decrees and be careful to keep my law*" (NIV). Since we cannot operate in the kingdom without the Holy Spirit, it follows that part of the process involved in entering that domain would be to receive the Spirit. His purpose in giving the Spirit is clear. It is so that we can obey his laws.

**Since we cannot operate in the kingdom
without the Holy Spirit, it follows that part
of the process involved in entering that
domain would be to receive the Spirit.**

The new birth described in John 3:3-5 must be understood in the context of the kingdom of God. Since the kingdom of God is the government of God, the new birth must be seen as the passage from self-rule, sin's control, and the domain of Satan (old government) to the rule of Christ (new government), and not simply a synonym for being saved. A careful comparison of Jesus's conversation with Nicodemus and his commission to his followers, including the way those followers applied his commission, verifies this conclusion and interpretation. The new birth is not fire insurance. It is a chance to live as a son of God—free of sin's control.

> **Jesus relates the new birth with the kingdom of God, therefore, it must be seen as the passage from self-rule and the domain of sin and Satan (old government) to the rule of Christ (new government), and not simply a synonym for being saved.**

The New Birth Process

Natural birth is a process. When the baby is ready to be born, it turns so its head faces towards the birth canal. Then, as the mother has contractions, the baby moves down the birth canal from the dark quiet of the womb into the light of the hospital or birthing room. In the next few moments, the baby will have its umbilical cord severed, and it will breathe. It will go from one form of life support to another. After this, the baby is usually cleaned up and placed next to its mother to be cuddled or fed.

The new birth is also a process. A person coming to Christ must turn toward God. He must believe in the Lord Jesus as he passes from the darkness to the light. His old life support must be severed in water baptism. He must breathe in the Holy Spirit. Then he must be cleaned up, loved, and nurtured (discipled).

There are four essential steps in the actual birth itself. These four things are foundational in the life and faith of a new believer. The four steps are as follows: repentance, faith toward God, water baptism, and being filled with the Holy Spirit. These steps will be explained in some detail because

15

of their extreme importance. I must remind the reader at this point that the new birth is a process of a change of government. Please keep that in mind. When someone comes to Christ, he is not just buying a ticket to heaven. It is a major change of life similar to marriage.

Marriage is a process. First, contact is made between two people (or two families, as is the case in some Eastern cultures). In the course of time, there is growing affection, or negotiations, that transpire. Then the couple becomes engaged or betrothed to be married (a decision). After this, there is a wedding ceremony in which the decision to marry is formally and publicly recognized and ratified. Subsequent to the nuptials is the very private act of intercourse that consummates the marriage. At what point in the process is one considered married?

If you have a formal ceremony but do not consummate the marriage, then it is not legal. Conversely, if you "consummate" without a wedding, then it is fornication, not marriage. It also stands to reason that if you don't decide to marry, then you won't. All the parts of this process are essential to arrive at the finished product. Both the illustrations of marriage and natural birth depict accurately for us what happens in the new birth.

Repentance is like the baby turning toward the birth canal or like the decision to date or become betrothed. Faith in Christ is like the coming into the light as the baby is born or like the formal decision to marry. Water baptism is the severing of the umbilical cord or the public wedding ceremony. Water baptism, severing the cord, and the wedding ceremony—all occur only once. Finally, the baby breathes (breath = *pneuma*, also means spirit), or the marriage is consummated by intercourse. These speak of being filled with the Holy Spirit. Like breathing or intercourse, "being filled" happens continually throughout your life (or marriage).

The four initial steps of seeing and entering the Rule of Christ:	
1. Repentance from acts leading to death	Seeing
2. Faith in the Lord Jesus Christ	
3. Immersion in water	Entering
4. Being filled with the Holy Spirit	

These four foundational steps are covered in detail in a companion volume to this book entitled *Building Your House on the Rock*. What follows is a quick overview.

Repentance

Repentance and faith are linked to seeing the kingdom of God. *Repentance* is our English word translated from a Greek word *metanoia*, meaning "to perceive afterwards." It is a function of perception. Basically, one could say repentance is seeing something in hindsight or in the context of relating to God, from God's point of view. When merged with the Hebrew understanding of repentance, we could accurately define repentance as a change of perception that leads to a change in behaviour. Repentance is more than saying, "I'm sorry." The key verse for repentance is Acts 26:20.

> *I preached that they should repent and turn to God*
> *and prove their repentance by their deeds.* **(NIV)**

We repent of sins. Imagine expecting new converts to prove their repentance. One of the problems we encounter today stems from a simplistic concept of repentance that says we can pray a general prayer like, *"Forgive me for my sins,"* or *"I confess that I am a sinner."* This shotgun approach does not help us change. Vague concepts of sin and vague confessions don't lead to action whereas specific confession focuses on where the action needs to take place. Better to say to your spouse, "Sorry, honey, I ridiculed you in front of your friend. In the future, I will try not to make jokes at your expense," than to say, "Sorry, honey, I think I said something that upset you." We need to clearly define what sin is.

> *I would not have known what sin was*
> *except through the law.* **(Rom. 7:7, NIV)**

Sin can be generally defined as anything against God and specifically defined as breaking the commandments of the law. The moral law of God reveals sins. *"Indeed I would not have known what sin was except through the law."* But there is something even more basic than breaking the rules. It is failing to acknowledge the Ruler. Many people simply fail to recognize God for who he is. Not only have they failed to obey his commands, they have forgotten who he is, or made him out to be different than he is, or denied his existence. This is why we so desperately need repentance. The law reveals not only the rules but also the character and nature of God. We need to see him as he is. We need a change of perception. He is Lord. He knows what is best. He has every right to rule. As we wrap our thinking around that concept, we will begin to align ourselves, our souls, and our lifestyles with that Lordship. As we begin to see God correctly, we will start to seek his government. This repentance is the initial step in seeing the kingdom of God.

We have often been reminded that Christianity is not a set of rules, but a relationship with God. Let me add a kingdom component to that revelation. Christianity is not a set of rules but a relationship with the Ruler.

Repentance begins with a change of mind that leads to a change of heart and a change of lifestyle. Repentance turns us away from sins and turns us towards faith in God. The change of heart could be called conversion. Conversion means to do a U-turn. Conversion is the visible portion of repentance coupled with believing.

> *Repent, then, and turn to God, so that your sins may be wiped out, that times of refreshing may come from the Lord, and that he may send the Christ, who has been appointed for you—even Jesus.* (Acts 3:19-20, NIV)

Faith

Faith towards God is the second part of seeing the government of God. Faith is absolutely necessary. *"But without faith it is impossible to please him: for he that cometh to God must believe that he is"* (Heb. 11:6, KJV). Faith is the most vital step in coming into the kingdom, for without it, you would not take the other steps. It functions at every step. We have often made it the only step, but it is significant that Peter stood on the day of Pentecost and told the crowd to repent and be baptized and receive the Holy Spirit. Faith was not emphasized; in fact, it was not even mentioned.

Believing in Jesus as LORD is where faith starts (Rom. 10:9-13). Too often, we point to a Saviour instead of pointing to a Lord. The Gospel of the kingdom points to a King. Faith without works is dead, or in other words, faith (i.e., that Jesus is Lord) without subsequent action (obeying that Lord) is not really faith. Acts 6:7 says, *"So the word of God spread. The number of disciples in Jerusalem increased rapidly, and a large number of priests became obedient to the faith"* (NIV). Faith is more than a mental concept. It is the springboard to obedience.

Faith without works is dead.
In other words, faith that Jesus is Lord
without subsequent action—
obeying His Lordship—is not really faith.

In Romans 10:10, we are told, *"With the mouth confession is made unto salvation"* (KJV). Faith must be verbally expressed, as well as acted upon. In John 3:16, we are told that whoever believes in him (the Son) will not perish. The Greek verb for *believe* is in the continuous tense. So it is really saying that whoever continues to believe in him will not perish. Faith is continual.

Throughout the New Testament, we are told to believe in the Lord Jesus. Not once in the context of seeing and entering the kingdom (becoming a disciple) are we told to receive Jesus into our heart. Jesus is a human. *"For there is . . . one mediator . . . the man [anthropos] Christ Jesus"* (1 Tim. 2:5, NIV). He is in heaven interceding for us. He occasionally visits the planet. He cannot live in our hearts, except by his Spirit. We are told to receive his Spirit (Acts 2:38). We believe in the Lord Jesus and receive the Holy Spirit. Teaching someone to receive Jesus into their heart only confuses things later.

Faith toward God includes
both trust and obedience.

Faith without appropriate action is useless.

The appropriate action when dealing with
Almighty God is to do exactly what he says
And trust that he is right.

Water Baptism

Together, water baptism and baptism with the Holy Spirit constitute the steps of entering the kingdom. By repentance and faith, we see the Lordship of Jesus, and now we obey that Lordship by doing what he commanded. Jesus commissioned us to make disciples by baptizing them. Baptism is a vital step in becoming a disciple.

It's interesting to note that when Jesus commissioned his followers to make disciples, he told them to teach the new disciples to obey all that he commanded. That is completely inclusive. Among the many instructions Jesus gave, baptism was one. Jesus highlights this one command, above the rest, as vital to the process of making a disciple. A disciple is someone who has left the kingdom or control of sin and entered the kingdom or rule of Christ. Water baptism represents the transfer from one kingdom to the other. It represents dying to the old way of life and to the old support system and being raised up in a new life. Water baptism identifies us with death, burial, and resurrection.

> *Or do you not know that as many of us as were baptized into Christ Jesus were baptized into His death? Therefore we were buried with Him through baptism into death, that just as Christ was raised from the dead by the glory of the Father, even so we also should walk in newness of life. For if we have been united together in the likeness of His death,* certainly we also shall be *in the likeness of His resurrection, knowing this, that our old man was crucified with* Him, *that the body of sin might be done away with, that we should no longer be slaves of sin. For he who has died has been freed from sin. Now if we died with Christ, we believe that we shall also live with Him, knowing that Christ, having been raised from the dead, dies no more. Death no longer has dominion over Him. For* the death *that He died, He died to sin once for all; but* the life *that He lives, He lives to God. Likewise you also, reckon yourselves to be dead indeed to sin, but alive to God in Christ Jesus our Lord.* (Rom. 6:3-11, NKJV)

Death frees us from the control of sin. In the story of Israel's deliverance from Egypt, you will recall that they crossed the Red Sea. This is symbolic of baptism. *"Moreover, brethren, I do not want you to be unaware that all our fathers were under the cloud, all passed through the sea, all were baptized into Moses in the cloud and in the sea"* (1 Cor. 10:1-2, NKJV). What died in the Red Sea during that great event? Pharaoh had sent his whole army after the Israelites to return them to slavery. His army represented the military might of Egypt. The ability of Egypt to force God's people back into slavery was killed that day. Sin's ability to force us back into its control is put to death in baptism. The blood of the Lamb saved the firstborn sons of Israel from the death angel. Baptism in the Red Sea saved Israel from being forced to return to serve Pharaoh. The water saved them from Pharaoh's (or sin's) control. *"Knowing this, that our old man was crucified with* Him, *that the body of sin might be done away with, that we should no longer be slaves of sin"* (Rom. 6:6, NKJV). We are no longer slaves to sin. That water "saves" may seem strange, but read 1 Peter 3:20-21:

> *God waited patiently in the days of Noah while the ark was being built. In it only a few people, eight in all, were saved through water, and this water symbolizes baptism that now saves you also—not the removal of dirt from the body but the pledge of a good conscience toward God. It saves you by the resurrection of Jesus Christ.* (NIV)

We have been taught that Jesus's death saves us. This is, of course, very true, but the Word also teaches that his resurrection saves us. Remember *saved* means "salvaged from sin," not just "safe from hell." The blood saves you from death and hell. The resurrection saves you from having to live according to the world's system of government. We are cut off from the flesh.

Crucifixion is the ultimate cutting off of the flesh. *"Knowing this, that our old man was crucified with Him, that the body of sin might be done away with,"* the whole body of sin is killed in crucifixion. The sign of the old covenant was circumcision. In circumcision, a part of the flesh was cut off. In the new covenant, circumcision is more complete. It is a circumcision of the heart and involves the cutting off of all flesh. The flesh must be cut off (killed) and buried, by immersion in water.

> *For in Christ all the fullness of the Deity lives in bodily form, and you have been given fullness in Christ, who is the Head over every power and authority. In him you were also circumcised, in*

the putting off of the sinful nature, not with a circumcision done by the hands of men but with the circumcision done by Christ, having been buried with him in baptism and raised with him through your faith in the power of God, who raised him from the dead. (Col. 2:9-12, NIV)

In the story of Israel's deliverance from Egypt and the story of Noah, water was involved in the transfer or deliverance of God's people from one world into the next. Israel came out of Egypt, into the wilderness and, ultimately, the Promised Land. Noah and his family were lifted out of a dying world and later deposited onto a new world. Water baptism is involved in our transfer from one kingdom to another.

He has delivered us from the power of darkness and conveyed us into the kingdom of the Son. (Col. 1:13)

Water baptism in a kingdom context has to do with entering the kingdom of God. It is the first outward sign of obedience or the evidence of faith. We are saved by faith, but faith without obedience is useless. In baptism, by faith, we identify with the death, burial, and resurrection of Christ. By faith, we are conveyed from the kingdom of darkness into the kingdom of light. By faith, we die to sin and are buried by immersion in water, and we emerge from the water in newness of life symbolizing the resurrection. How do we know that our old man was crucified with him? We know by faith.

You might have such questions as the following: *"Does immersion in water convey us from one kingdom to the other or is it just symbolic of it?" "Is it an actual circumcision or just symbolic?" "Is it an actual crucifixion and burial or just symbolic?"* Personally, I think there is actually more going on than we have realized. I believe that immersion in water is a physical act with spiritual consequences. I believe water baptism cuts us off from sin's ability to force us back into serving it. You can still choose to serve sin if you want to, but it cannot force you back into slavery. I believe that the reason Jesus mentioned baptism when he told his followers to make disciples (Matt. 28:18-20), was because it represents, better than any other picture, death to the old way of life and a new beginning. Read Romans 6:2-11 a couple more times:

> *Or do you not know that as many of us as were baptized into Christ Jesus were baptized into His death? Therefore we were buried with Him through baptism into death, that just as Christ was raised from the dead by the glory of the Father, even so we also should walk in newness of life. For if we have been united together in the likeness of His death, certainly we also shall be in the likeness of His resurrection, knowing this, that our old man was crucified with Him, that the body of sin might be done away with, that we should no longer be slaves of sin. For he who has died has been freed from sin. Now if we died with Christ, we believe that we shall also live with Him, knowing that Christ, having been raised from the dead, dies no more. Death no longer has dominion over Him. For the death that He died, He died to sin once for all; but the life that He lives, He lives to God. Likewise you also, reckon yourselves to be dead indeed to sin, but alive to God in Christ Jesus our Lord.* (NKJV)

Baptism in the Holy Spirit

The fourth step of initiation or new birth into the government of God, or rule of Christ, is to be filled with the Holy Spirit. In our comparison to natural birth, this is analogous to breathing. The Greek word *pneuma* means breath or spirit. Breathing is, of course, essential to life. The Holy Spirit is given to us, to empower us to prosper in the kingdom of God. The Holy Spirit is life to us.

> *Therefore, there is now no condemnation for those who are in Christ Jesus, because through Christ Jesus the law of the Spirit of life set me free from the law of sin and death. For what the law was powerless to do in that it was weakened by the sinful nature, God did by sending his own Son in the likeness of sinful man to be a sin offering. And so he condemned sin in sinful man, in order that the righteous requirements of the law might be fully met in us, who do not live*

according to the sinful nature but according to the Spirit. Those who live according to the sinful nature have their minds set on what that nature desires; but those who live in accordance with the Spirit have their minds set on what the Spirit desires. The mind of sinful man is death, but the mind controlled by the Spirit is life and peace; the sinful mind is hostile to God. It does not submit to God's law, nor can it do so. Those controlled by the sinful nature cannot please God. You, however, are controlled not by the sinful nature but by the Spirit, if the Spirit of God lives in you. And if anyone does not have the Spirit of Christ, he does not belong to Christ. But if Christ is in you, your body is dead because of sin, yet your spirit is alive because of righteousness. And if the Spirit of him who raised Jesus from the dead is living in you, he who raised Christ from the dead will also give life to your mortal bodies through his Spirit, who lives in you. (Rom. 8:1-11, NIV)

The Holy Spirit is more than life to us—he is Lord. He is the administrator of God's kingdom on earth. When God designed the new covenant, he decided to write the law into our hearts and minds. The law—the Ten Commandments—was given at Mount Sinai on the day of Pentecost, fifty days after the Passover which activated Israel's release from Egypt. That law was, in effect, God's government. In the new covenant, on the day of Pentecost, the Spirit was given. He is God's government. The kingdom of God is the rule of Christ, the Holy Spirit.

Modern teaching that is antinomian in nature (all grace and no law) has failed to convey the vital importance of Romans 8:4—the righteous requirements of the law might be fully met in us. The example of Israel more than adequately conveys mankind's total inability to obey God's laws. We admit that we ourselves cannot fully meet all the righteous requirements of the law. The truth is, we cannot, but the Holy Spirit in us can.

God found something wrong with the first covenant. He found fault with the people. There was nothing wrong with the law he authored. It was man's inability to comply with that good law that led God to design a new covenant. As you read about this in Hebrews 8, note that with the new covenant, he takes the law (the same law) that was external and internalizes it by writing it on two new tablets, our mind and our heart. His purpose is clear. He wants us to know him as Lord. Lord is who he is.

> *For if that first* covenant *had been faultless, then no place would have been sought for a second. Because finding fault with them, He says:* "Behold, the days are coming, says the LORD, when I will make a new covenant with the house of Israel and with the house of Judah—not according to the covenant that I made with their fathers in the day when I took them by the hand to lead them out of the land of Egypt; because they did not continue [remain faithful] in My covenant, and I disregarded them, says the LORD. For this is the covenant that I will make with the house of Israel after those days, says the Lord: I will put My laws in their mind and write them on their hearts; and I will be their God, and they shall be My people. None of them shall teach his neighbour, and none his brother, saying, 'Know the LORD,' for all shall know Me, from the least of them to the greatest of them. For I will be merciful to their unrighteousness, and their sins and their lawless deeds I will remember no more." In that He says, "A new covenant," He has made the first obsolete. Now what is becoming obsolete and growing old is ready to vanish away. (Heb. 8:7-13, NKJV)

> *A new heart also will I give you, and a new spirit will I put within you: and I will take away the stony heart out of your flesh, and I will give you an heart of flesh. And I will put my spirit within you, and cause you to walk in my statutes, and ye shall keep my judgments, and do them. And ye shall dwell in the land that I gave to your fathers; and ye shall be my people, and I will be your God.* (Ezek. 36:26-28, KJV)

The NIV says, *"I will put my Spirit in you and move you to follow my decrees and be careful to keep my laws"* (Ezek. 36:27). God desires obedient children. He puts his Spirit into us to empower us to keep his laws. The letter to the Romans says it this way: *"The mind controlled by the Spirit is life and peace*" (Rom. 8:6, NIV). Yes, as bad as it may sound, God is into mind control. Stop and think about it. Either sin (or the flesh) controls your thinking, or God does. Take your pick. Jesus chose to let the Spirit control his thinking.

It seems that what God wants to do is reprogram our thinking so that we can live and act like Jesus. He gives us files to download into our hard drive. (He writes his laws in our minds and hearts.) Then he sends the Holy Spirit, who gives us power to run those programs. There is much more to say about the Holy Spirit and his baptism: how you are filled, when you are filled, and what happens when you are filled. Since I cover this in the companion volume *Building Your House on the Rock: Kingdom Foundations*, I won't go into all the details now. In the *Foundations* book, I cover all the conversion experiences in the book of Acts and demonstrate that every disciple was filled with the Holy Spirit. Since the kingdom of God is the rule of the Holy Spirit, and since the Spirit is in us, it makes sense that to initially enter that realm requires that we be baptized with the Spirit.

**Since we cannot operate in the kingdom
without the Holy Spirit, it follows that part
of the process involved in entering that
domain would be to receive the Spirit.**

4

~ PATTERN FOR CHANGE ~

Zelzah, Tabor and Gibeah

The new birth has been explained as coming under new management. You are freed from sin's control and have entered into a new life under the control of the Holy Spirit. At this point, you are a brand-new creature in Christ. You are a newborn infant, a baby. In time, you will grow up and be about the Father's business. Entering into the kingdom can occur quickly—in a matter of minutes. Growing up spiritually takes more time. The new birth transformed your spirit, now God wants to transform your mind.

You enter the Rule of Christ via the new birth, and therefore enter the family business as a son. The Greek word for this is *teknon*. It means you are a child by birth or adoption. As a son, you are entitled to the benefits of sonship including access to Father. You are not a servant or a slave that must earn the master's approval. You are a member of the family. At the same time, you are an immature son. You are not a fully developed mature son. The Greek word for mature son is *huios*. A mature son reflects the same character as the Father. When you are a mature son, you will look like and act like Jesus.

Our goal, therefore, is to grow up as sons into maturity or into Christ, *"to the measure of the stature of the fullness of Christ; that we should no longer be [immature] children . . . but . . . may grow up in all things into Him, who is the head—Christ"* (Eph 4:13-15, NKJV).

27

In order to grow up or mature, we need to be transformed in our soul or mind (Rom. 12:2). We need to work out the salvation of our soul with fear and trembling (Phil. 2:12). We need to be changed in our thinking. The Bible says to be carnally minded is death, but to be spiritually minded is life. Carnally minded means to have our thinking dominated by the flesh.

For those who live according to the flesh set their minds on the things of the flesh, but those who live according to the Spirit, the things of the Spirit. For to be carnally minded is death, but to be spiritually minded is life and peace. Because the carnal mind is enmity against God; for it is not subject to the law of God, nor indeed can be. So then, those who are in the flesh cannot please God. But you are not in the flesh but in the Spirit, if indeed the Spirit of God dwells in you. Now if anyone does not have the Spirit of Christ, he is not His. And if Christ is in you, the body is dead because of sin, but the Spirit is life because of righteousness. But if the Spirit of Him who raised Jesus from the dead dwells in you, He who raised Christ from the dead will also give life to your mortal bodies through His Spirit who dwells in you. Therefore, brethren, we are debtors—not to the flesh, to live according to the flesh. For if you live according to the flesh you will die; but if by the Spirit you put to death the deeds of the body, you will live. For as many as are led by the Spirit of God, these are sons of God. For you did not receive the spirit of bondage again to fear, but you received the Spirit of adoption by whom we cry out, "Abba, Father." The Spirit Himself bears witness with our spirit that we are children of God, and if children, then heirs—heirs of God and joint heirs with Christ, if indeed we suffer with Him, *that we may also be glorified together.* (Rom. 8:5-17, NKJV).

So we see that the initial steps in coming under the government of God involve being made dead to sin and alive spiritually, but the steps we take in living under the government of God involve dying to the flesh. The flesh must die. Flesh doesn't mean body or physical attributes. Flesh means desires arising from our human nature or human thinking rather than coming from the divine nature. These desires must die, and our thinking must be reprogrammed.

For example, all your life you may have been told you are useless, no good, and unacceptable. These ideas exist in your carnal thinking, not in God's mind. God created you and has positive thoughts of acceptance and love towards you. One day, God prompts you to say something or do something, and you think, "I can't possibly do that—I am useless, no good, and unacceptable." God says you can do all things through the anointing but you think, "No, I can't." In order to brightly reflect the glory of God, we must allow God to put such carnal thinking to death so that we will be like Jesus. Jesus did what the Father told him to without reflecting negatively on his circumstances or abilities.

Your mind is like a computer. It has a treasury of knowledge and experience stored in it. This wasn't programmed in a day. It has taken years to program your brain. The reprogramming of the mind will take years as well. It will require consistent and persistent work. Certain files will need to be erased. For example the "When I get angry I smack someone in the face" file will need to be deleted and replaced with the "Be angry and sin not" file. The new files are in the Word of God. They are entered into the "hard drive" of our thinking as we read, hear, study, meditate on, and, not forgetting, "do" the scriptures—both the Old Testament and the New Testament. This reprogramming will change us into a different person.

King Saul had an opportunity to change into a different man. His experience gives us what I call a pattern for change. King Saul represents for us our flesh nature, therefore we can relate to Saul. The flesh needs to give way to the Spirit.

A Pattern for Change

> Then Samuel took a flask of oil and poured it on his head, and kissed him and said: "Is it not because the LORD has anointed you commander over His inheritance? When you have departed from me today, you will find two men by Rachel's tomb in the territory of Benjamin at Zelzah; and they will say to you, 'The donkeys which you went to look for have been found. And now your father has ceased caring about the donkeys and is worrying about you, saying, "What shall I do about my son?"'Then you shall go on forward from there and come to the terebinth tree of Tabor. There three men

going up to God at Bethel will meet you, one carrying three young goats, another carrying three loaves of bread, and another carrying a skin of wine. And they will greet you and give you two loaves *of bread, which you shall receive from their hands. After that you shall come to the hill of God where the Philistine garrison* is. *And it will happen, when you have come there to the city, that you will meet a group of prophets coming down from the high place with a stringed instrument, a tambourine, a flute, and a harp before them; and they will be prophesying. Then the Spirit of the LORD will come upon you, and you will prophesy with them and be turned into another man. And let it be, when these signs come to you,* that *you do as the occasion demands; for God* is *with you. You shall go down before me to Gilgal; and surely I will come down to you to offer burnt offerings* and *make sacrifices of peace offerings. Seven days you shall wait, till I come to you and show you what you should do.*" (1 Sam. 10:1-8, NKJV)

God has anointed us with the Holy Spirit and enabled us to share in the inheritance. We have been given authority to be kings and priests. We have been qualified.

[W]e . . . ask that you may be filled with the knowledge of His will in all wisdom and spiritual understanding; that you may walk worthy of the Lord, fully pleasing Him, *being fruitful in every good work and increasing in the knowledge of God; strengthened with all might, according to His glorious power, for all patience and longsuffering with joy; giving thanks to the Father who has qualified us to be partakers of the inheritance of the saints in the light. He has delivered us from the power of darkness and conveyed us into the kingdom of the Son of His love, in whom we have redemption through His blood.* (Col. 1:9-14, KJV)

Saul was directed by Samuel to go to three places: Zelzah, Tabor, and Gilgal. *Zelzah* means "noon" and represents an appointed time. *Tabor* means "purity" and represents freedom from pollution of distraction. *Gilgal* means "hill" and represents a geographic place. I believe that God wants us to set a time and find a place free of distractions, where we can have a quiet time with him. It is in these quiet times (devotions), by spending time with him, that we will be changed.

At these three locations, three events took place. These three events can represent activities that we incorporate into a devotional time.

At Zelzah, near Rachel's tomb, Saul was to meet two men. *"[T]hey will say to you, 'The donkeys which you went to look for have been found. And now your father has ceased caring about the donkeys and is worrying about you, saying, "What shall I do about my son?"'"* (1 Sam. 10:2, KJV). What is very significant is that this occurs by Rachel's tomb. Rachel was the beloved wife of Jacob.

Jacob, as you may recall, had four women in his life. Two wives and their maids all gave Jacob children. Rachel was his favourite. This is where she was buried. This is where you and I must bury what we treasure most. We must die to our cherished desires and plans. We must surrender agendas and goals to the Lord. Rather than praying to God about the things we want, we should pray, *"Not my will but thy will be done today."* We let what we want to do die and consult him about what he wants us to do today.

God has something to say to you in this quiet time. He wants to say, "Don't worry about the donkeys." Saul was out looking for his father's donkeys. He was out there working for his father. God, our Father, wants to say, "I am more concerned about you than your mission. Let's spend some quality time together." In our time alone with God, as well as surrendering our favourite desires to him, we need to listen to him.

Donkeys can represent our busyness, our mission, our work, ministry, or even the things that we chase after when we should be chasing after God. Stop chasing the donkeys and smell the presence of God. Put those things you love into the tomb. Don't worry. God can resurrect them if he wants to. God wants to convey his special care for you, so take time to listen.

At the great tree of Tabor, Saul was to meet three men. *"They will greet you and give you two loaves of bread"* (1 Sam. 10:4, NKJV). Bread represents the Word of God. Saul was to accept two out of three loaves. Some Bibles have three sections: the Old Testament, the Apocryhpha, and the New Testament. We accept two—the Old and New testaments. Christians need to eat both loaves, not just nibble away on the New. The Old Testament provides the only basis or foundation on which to better understand the teaching of the New. The early church had only one Bible—the Old Testament. They changed the world in which they lived.

In our quiet time with God—after dying to fleshly desires, giving him control of our daily agenda and listening to him—we input the Word of God into our spirits and minds. We reprogram the hard drive. Give us this day our daily bread. Just like our bodies want to eat food, our spirits want to eat spirit food. Why do we consider feeding our bodies three or four times per day normal, but feeding our spirits once a day a chore? It is not legalism to feed our spirit once or twice a day. It is vital if we are to prosper spiritually. *"Let the word of Christ dwell in you richly in all wisdom; teaching and admonishing one another in psalms and hymns and spiritual songs, singing with grace in your hearts to the Lord"* (Col. 3:16, KJV).

In Gibeah, Saul was to meet a procession of singing prophesying prophets. *"The Spirit of the LORD will come upon you, and you will prophesy with them and be turned into another man"* (1 Sam. 10:6, NKJV) The most important event was that the Spirit came upon him. During our quiet time, we should ask God to fill us afresh with the Holy Spirit. We need to be filled not just once but constantly, continually, or daily.

You will note that the prophets were singing and worshipping with music. During your time alone with God, consider worshipping and praising him using song. Make a joyful noise unto the Lord. *"Be filled with the Spirit; speaking to yourselves in psalms and hymns and spiritual songs, singing and making melody in your heart to the Lord; Giving thanks always for all things unto God and the Father in the name of our Lord Jesus Christ"* (Eph. 5:18-20, KJV). Some suggest that you could worship first before prayer or reading the Word. The important thing is to get filled with the Spirit. The overflow of that are singing, rejoicing, and thanksgiving.

Samuel told Saul that he would prophesy with these men immediately after being filled with the Spirit. That, of course, agrees with the Book of Acts, where people filled with the Spirit prophesied or spoke in tongues. We should pray in the Spirit.

There is another important application of this. The Spirit of prophesy is the testimony of Jesus. Revelations 19:10 says, *"I am your fellow servant, and of your brethren who have the testimony of Jesus. Worship God! For the testimony [witness] of Jesus is the spirit of prophecy"* (NKJV). Jesus said in Acts

1:8, *"You will receive power when the Holy Spirit comes on you; and you will be my witnesses"* (NIV). We need to be filled with the Spirit to witness.

We should consider that our quiet time with God is a preparation for doing what he has called us to do, which is to build the family business—to seek and save the lost—to make disciples of all nations. We need to be filled with the Spirit to receive power and to be witnesses. The Holy Spirit also provides boldness and wisdom. The gifts of the Spirit enable us to do effective evangelism, and the fruit of the Spirit enables us to walk the walk. The leadership of the Spirit guides us into all truth. The Spirit intercedes through us as we pray in the Spirit. During this quiet time with God, it would be well to pray in the Spirit (tongues) for a while and also pray with understanding for people that need to become disciples. Pray for wisdom. Pray for divine appointments with people you can witness to, encourage, or heal.

Saul is told that once these signs are fulfilled, he can do whatever his hand finds to do—do as the occasion demands, for God is with him. This sounds like you can now do your own thing, but stop and consider this. You have died to the flesh by putting your agenda in the tomb. You have listened to the Father. You have filled your mind with the Word of God, and you have been filled afresh with the Holy Spirit. You have spent some time worshipping the Lord and praying in tongues. You have asked for divine appointments and prayed for the lost. You are focused. You are empowered. You are anointed with power to go forth and do good, healing all those who are oppressed by the devil, for God is with you. You are ready to obey Colossians 3:17: *"And whatsoever ye do in word or deed, do all in the name of the Lord Jesus"* (KJV).

The Holy Spirit enables us to change into a different person—someone who looks and acts like Jesus, the prototype. *"God anointed Jesus of Nazareth with the Holy Spirit and with power, who went about doing good and healing all who were oppressed by the devil, for God was with Him"* (Acts 10:38, NKJV). Daily devotions won't do us much good if they don't affect what we do with our hands. In other words, after spending quality time with God building faith, go out and do practical things with your hands that show the love of God to this dying world.

Finally, Samuel instructed the new king to wait seven days for further instructions. *"You shall go down before me to Gilgal; and surely I will come down to you to offer burnt offerings* and *make sacrifices of peace offerings. Seven days you shall wait, till I come to you and show you what you should do"* (1 Sam. 10:8, NKJV). You and I need to learn how to hear from God and how to be led by the Spirit. We need to become intimate with the Father, obedient to the Lord Jesus, and filled with the Holy Spirit. This is our vital necessity. We also need to hear God speak through anointed men and women of God, especially those God has given to us as leaders, mentors, or instructors. *"Obey those who rule over you, and be submissive, for they watch out for your souls"* (Heb. 13:17, NKJV). Jesus has given us various instructors to help us mature (Eph. 4:11-14). We need to listen to them, as well as have devotions.

> *And He Himself gave some* to be *apostles, some prophets, some evangelists, and some pastors and teachers, for the equipping of the saints for the work of ministry, for the edifying of the body of Christ, till we all come to the unity of the faith and of the knowledge of the Son of God, to a perfect man, to the measure of the stature of the fullness of Christ; that we should no longer be children.* (Eph. 4:11-14, NKJV)

This chapter was written to give you a pattern for daily devotions. Many useful patterns exist. The Lord's Prayer and the Tabernacle of Moses also serve as patterns. You can try a variety of them. You can pray the Word of God. I've given you Colossians 1:9-14 in this section as an example. The essential truth is simply this: If you want to grow up in the kingdom, you need to die to self (to the flesh), learn the Word of God, and be constantly filled with the Holy Spirit. You need to grow in faith by reprogramming the mind with the Word and by doing works of faith.

5

~ REIGNING IN LIFE ~

The Gift of Righteousness and the Abundance of Grace

Those who receive abundance of grace and of the gift of righteousness will reign in life through the One, Jesus Christ. (Rom. 5:17, NKJV)

God has called us to be overcomers. We are to reign in life. God put Adam on the planet to have dominion. Now that we have looked at and emphasized God's sovereignty—his rule, his kingdom—let's look at our ruling and reigning in life through him.

We are called to sonship and partnership with the Almighty. In calling us to sonship, God the Father is actually revealing how much like him we really are. Think about all the potential in that remark. We are created in his image. We start in the kingdom as sons, no less. Jesus, our elder brother, was the prototype. Jesus reconciled us to the Father. The word *father* implies a relationship, where he is the nurturing, loving authority, responsible for our care and development. He is provider and has a wealth of wisdom and experience we can learn from. As sons, we have a sense of belonging, a sense of gratitude, of respect, and of wanting to be like him. Children must obey their parents, but it isn't military school. It is family. Children are accepted and loved from the start and eventually learn to take responsibilities, which at times, and in certain cultures, include the family business.

Since God is Lord by his very nature and function, part of being like him is to rule and reign in life. Adam was given dominion. Adam ruled in conjunction with the Creator. Adam tended the garden. God owned the garden, and Adam was in charge of it. Adam had dominion within the confines of God's sovereignty. When Adam rebelled against God's Lordship, he lost his authority to tend the garden. Jesus restores what Adam lost. We become one with Christ when we recognize and accept his authority and Lordship over our lives. We were given free will, so when we give over that will freely to Jesus, he calls us into partnership with him. We are partners with Almightiness. Bear in mind, of course, that he is the senior partner.

Before we entered the kingdom of God, we were outsiders, sinners, under the wrath of God, and destined to hell. Two words described our condition: *cut off*. After we entered the kingdom, we were insiders, adopted, fellow heirs with Jesus, and partners with God. Two words describe our condition: *well connected*. Before we look at how we reign through the abundance of grace and of the gift of righteousness, let's take a brief look at whom we are connected to. We are partners with the following.

Partnered with the Lord

Yahweh-Jireh—"The LORD Will Provide" (Gen. 22:14, NIV). This was the name given to the location where God provided a ram for Abraham to sacrifice in the place of Isaac. This name is a testimony to God's deliverance. It actually means God is provision.

Yahweh-Rapha—"For I am the LORD that healeth thee" (Exod. 15:26, KJV). God is health.

Yahweh-Nissi—"The LORD is my Banner" (Exod. 17:15, NIV). Moses ascribed this name to God after a victory over the Amalekites. The name of God was considered a banner under which Israel could rally for victory. The Lord's name was the battle cry. God is victory.

Yahweh-Mekaddesh—"The Lord who sanctifies" (Ex. 31:13, NKJV). Holiness is the central revelation of God's character. God calls for a people who are set apart. He is sanctification.

Yahweh-Shalom—"The LORD is Peace" (Judg. 6:24, NIV). This was the name of the altar that Gideon built at Ophrah signifying that God brings well-being, not death, to his people. God is peace, prosperity, and wholeness.

Yahweh-Sabaoth—"The LORD of hosts" (1 Sam. 1:3, KJV; Jer. 11:20, KJV; compare 1 Sam. 17:45, KJV). This can also be rendered "The Lord Almighty." It represents God's power over the nations and was closely tied to Shiloh, to the ark of the covenant, and to prophecy. The title designates God as King and ruler of Israel, its armies, its temple, and of all the universe. God is almightiness. He is our strength.

Yahweh-Rohi—"The LORD is my Shepherd" (Ps. 23:1, KJV). God is the One who provides loving care for his people. God is loving care.

Yahweh-Tsidkenu—"The LORD [is] Our Righteousness" (Jer. 23:5-6; 33:16, NIV). This was the name Jeremiah gave to God, the Righteous King, who would rule over Israel after the return from captivity. He would establish a new kingdom of justice. God is our righteousness.

Yahweh-Shammah—"The LORD is There" (Ezek. 48:35, NIV). This is the name of God associated with the restoration of Jerusalem, God's dwelling place. *"Lo, I am with you always."*

Yahweh means *"I am that I am."*

> I am provision.
> I am health.
> I am victory.
> I am strength.
> I am holiness.
> I am peace (wholeness, prosperity).
> I am loving care.
> I am righteousness.
> I am there for you.

We are partnered with this particular powerful God. We can rule over sickness because our Partner is health. We can rule over poverty because our Partner is provision. We can rule over enemies because our Partner has triumphed. He is victory. We can rule over sin and temptation because we are partnered with righteousness and sanctification. We can rule over loneliness, depression, rejection, shame, bitterness, pride, and even death, all because of Jesus. He who knew no sin became sin for us that we might become the righteousness of God in Christ. We can rule and reign because of this gift of righteousness. We can rule and reign in life because he has given us the very presence of God Almighty in our spirits. He put his Spirit into us to empower us to prosper in all his ways.

Basically, we reign in life through two gifts: the abundance of grace and the gift of righteousness. *"Those who receive abundance of grace and of the gift of righteousness will reign in life through the One, Jesus Christ"* (Rom. 5:17, NKJV).

The Abundance of Grace

After doing a teaching series on the kingdom or government of God, I often minister prophetically according to 1 Corinthians: *"But everyone who prophesies speaks to men for their strengthening, encouragement and comfort . . . . For you can all prophesy in turn so that everyone may be instructed and encouraged"* (1 Cor. 14:3, 14:31, NIV). I think that after being taught on the Lordship of Jesus, it is good to encourage the saints in the love and grace of Jesus. The folks really need it after hearing me teach for ten hours or more on the rule of Christ. In some countries, the results are amazing. When God speaks to people who might have never heard personal prophecy before, and when they hear that God really cares about them and loves them, it releases blessing.

On one such teaching trip in the Ukraine, I realized that the saints there were not too familiar with the concept of his grace. They didn't really comprehend that they were (past tense) saved by grace. As I have traveled around and talked to various Christians, I've found that it is indicative of many saints that they don't know what grace really is. Either they are somewhat ignorant of the concept and tend to be legalistic, as they were in the Ukraine, or they see grace as all mercy, kindness, and forgiveness.

Grace is not mercy. It goes way beyond mercy. Grace is not the absence of rules or standards. Grace has been defined as unmerited favour, which doesn't really do the word justice, but it's a start. The problem with this definition is that most people see the unmerited part and skip over what favour is. Unmerited means undeserved or unearned, but to say that you don't need to do anything to get grace is an exaggeration. Grace is given to the humble and not to the proud. That is a criterion, is it not? In actual fact, grace is available to everyone, but the proud don't think they need it. The humble ask for it and are given it.

The real meat of "unmerited favour" is not the *unmerited* part but the *favour* part. Favour from God is rich and dynamic. Insight into God's kind of favour can be gleaned from Mary's experience with Gabriel in Luke 1:26-38, 45. Please note the words *favour* and *blessing*. Also, see the part the Holy Spirit plays.

> *And in the sixth month the angel Gabriel was sent from God unto a city of Galilee, named Nazareth, to a virgin espoused to a man whose name was Joseph, of the house of David; and the virgin's name was Mary. And the angel came in unto her, and said, Hail, thou that art highly favoured, the Lord is with thee: blessed art thou among women. And when she saw him, she was troubled at his saying, and cast in her mind what manner of salutation this should be. And the angel said unto her, Fear not, Mary: for thou hast found favour with God. And, behold, thou shalt conceive in thy womb, and bring forth a son, and shalt call his name JESUS. He shall be great, and shall be called the Son of the Highest: and the Lord God shall give unto him the throne of his father David: And He shall reign over the house of Jacob for ever; and of his kingdom there shall be no end. Then said Mary unto the angel, How shall this be, seeing I know not a man? And the angel answered and said unto her, The Holy Ghost shall come upon thee, and the power of the Highest shall overshadow thee: therefore also that Holy thing which shall be born of thee shall be called the Son of God. And, behold, thy cousin Elisabeth, she hath also conceived a son in her old age: and this is the sixth month with her, who was called barren. For with God nothing shall be impossible. And Mary said, Behold the handmaid of the Lord; be it unto me according to thy word. And the angel departed from her.*
> (Luke 1:26-38, KJV)

> *And blessed is she that believed: for there shall be a performance of those things which were told her from the Lord.* (Luke 1:45, KJV)

Mary was favoured, and Mary was blessed. "Favour" is derived from the Greek word *charis*, meaning "divine influence." Mary was to come under divine influence. The word "blessed" is translated from either of two

Greek words. The word "blessed" in verse 28 *("Hail, thou that art highly favoured, the Lord is with thee: blessed art thou among women")*, is *eulogio*, meaning "to speak well of," or "to prosper." Its counterpart in Hebrew is the word *barak*. *Barak* means "to endue with power for success, prosperity, fecundity (fruitfulness), and longevity." Abraham was blessed by God, and his blessings come to us. The *barak* blessing is basically a gift from God.

"Blessed" *Barak*—**means to endue with power for success, prosperity, fecundity, and longevity.**

The word *blessed* in verse 45 *("And blessed is she that believed")* is the Greek word *makarious*, which means "supremely blest, fortunate, to be envied, and well off." This is a superblessing! Its counterpart in Hebrew is the word *ashar* which means happy, to be envied and fortunate. To get the *ashar* or *makarious* blessing, one must do something, as in Psalm 1:1: *"Blessed is the man that walks not in the counsel of the ungodly, nor stands in the path of sinners, nor sits in the seat of the scornful."(NKJV)* One must obey God's counsel (believe God) to acquire the superblessing.

Mary was highly favoured and blessed. She was to come under divine influence and to be endued with power to prosper. She was to have a child who would be King. When Mary asks how all this will happen, she is told, *"The Holy Ghost shall come upon you, and the power of the Highest shall overshadow you."* In other words, God is going to do it with his power through the agency of the Spirit. Mary responds by agreeing with God. She gives her volitional surrender, and by saying yes to the Word of God, she releases the blessing of God in her life.

Between the words "highly favoured" and "blessed" comes the dynamite reality of what favour from God really is—the Lord is with thee.

Favour is the empowering presence of God.

Grace is the generous gift of the indwelling presence of the Holy Spirit, with his divine influence and empowerment—for success, prosperity, fecundity (fruitfulness), and longevity—that we access by faith and humility. Grace, to a disciple of Christ, is divine power coming from the indwelling presence of the Holy Spirit. We are saved by grace, not by works. Works speak of human effort and energy. Grace speaks of divine effort and energy. Grace is not mercy. It is power. Because of his great mercy, he gives us grace.

Grace = the power of God that comes from the indwelling presence of the Holy Spirit.

Grace is the generous gift of the indwelling presence of the Holy Spirit, with His divine influence and empowerment—for success, prosperity, fecundity, and longevity—that we access by faith and humility.

Grace, in the form of the indwelling Spirit, is given to us to enable us to obey God's commands. *"I will put my Spirit in you and move you to follow my decrees and be careful to keep my laws"* (Ezek. 36:27, NIV). It is in obeying his commands that we rule in life. Remember the great commission in Matthew 28 says, to *teach them to obey my commands.* The only way disciples can obey God is by his grace. Reigning in life is not simply having God cut you some slack. Reigning in life means doing the will of God. We are able to do it in his divine strength, just like Jesus did. Jesus was full of grace and truth. He was also full of the Holy Spirit. The Spirit is the Spirit of truth and the Spirit of grace. Jesus was full of divine influence and power. Grace flows from the Spirit. *"I will put my Spirit in you and move you to follow my decrees and be careful to keep my laws."*

The Gift of Righteousness

> *"[T]hose who receive abundance of grace and of the gift of righteousness will reign in life through the One, Jesus Christ"* (Rom. 5:17, NKJV).

The second gift of God that empowers us to reign in life is the gift of righteousness. I have already defined righteousness as a gift and a fruit in chapter 2. The gift of righteousness justified us before God. It is, of course, one of the greatest benefits of the cross.

"For [God] made [Jesus] who knew no sin to be sin for us, that we might become the righteousness of God in Him" (2 Cor. 5:21, NKJV).

Unfortunately, few of us have fully realized the significance of this imputed righteousness. We can come boldly to the throne of grace. Note that grace sits on a throne. We can come confidently to the throne of grace (divine influence, power, and wealth) because from God's point of view, we are righteous. What hinder us from reigning in life are the sin and the unworthiness we feel when we sin. Although we may come to God, we often don't, because we think that we don't really merit coming. Our hearts condemn us. We just don't think we are good enough. Our hearts may condemn us, but God does not condemn us.

The fact is, we aren't good enough, but Jesus has made us to be righteous. The problem is we don't trust—I mean, really trust—that his imputed righteousness will do it for us. I am the righteousness of God in Christ regardless of how I feel. To reign in life will require that we live by faith in the Word, not by feelings. We must make a quality decision to believe God. If God says I am, I am.

> **To reign in life will require that we live by faith in the Word not by feelings. We must make a quality decision to believe God's Word.**

Abraham believed God, and it was imputed unto him for righteousness: and he was called the Friend of God. (James 2:23, KJV)

That as sin hath reigned unto death, even so might grace reign through righteousness unto eternal life by Jesus Christ our Lord. (Rom. 5:21, KJV)

Grace, or divine empowerment, reigns through righteousness. The two work together. Jesus has a scepter by which he rules. It is a scepter of righteousness. *"But unto the Son he saith, Thy throne, O God, is for ever and ever: a sceptre of righteousness is the sceptre of thy kingdom"* (Heb. 1:8, KJV). You and I will never think of wielding that scepter or joining into partnership with Almightiness while we wallow in doubt as to our worthiness.

My son has no real problem asking to borrow the car because he knows who he is. My daughter also expects to borrow the car. She knows who she is. They both have their own sets of keys to the car. They both have valid driver's licenses. They feel quite free to use the car because they think it belongs to the family. And something that they perceive as belonging to the family, they see as belonging to them. They take ownership. We need to take ownership of what God has given us. We are his family. He has given us righteousness, and it is a scepter to be used.

Righteousness is also a breastplate that protects our vital organs.

> *Wherefore take unto you the whole armour of God, that ye may be able to withstand in the evil day, and having done all, to stand. Stand therefore, having your loins girt about with truth, and having on the breastplate of righteousness; And your feet shod with the preparation of the gospel of peace; Above all, taking the shield of faith, wherewith ye shall be able to quench all the fiery darts of the wicked. And take the helmet of salvation, and the sword of the Spirit, which is the word of God: Praying always with all prayer and supplication in the Spirit, and watching thereunto with all perseverance and supplication for all saints. (Eph. 6:13-18, KJV)*

Ruling in life will require battling in prayer. We need to know what the breastplate is and what it does.

Righteousness is a gift we receive by faith and we use by faith. It means we are justified before God and can come before his throne to obtain grace. God does not condemn us, but sometimes our own hearts condemn us. Therefore, we must make a quality decision to believe God's Word over our own feelings if we are to reign in life.

Being Great in God's Kingdom

> *Ye know that they which are accounted to rule over the Gentiles exercise lordship over them; and their great ones exercise authority*

upon them. But so shall it not be among you: but whosoever will be great among you, shall be your minister: And whosoever of you will be the chiefest, shall be servant of all. (Mark 10:42-44, KJV)

But whoever practices and teaches these commands will be called great in the kingdom of heaven. (Matt. 5:19, NIV)

I want to be great in the kingdom of God. I can do that by being a servant of all and by doing and teaching even the least of the commandments. That is exactly what Jesus did. He allowed God to rule his life, and by doing so, ruled in life over sin and sickness. We can do likewise. We rule and reign in life by faith, humility, and love. Love fulfills the law, and faith upholds the law. Jesus as a mature son (*huios*) accurately reflected the nature of the Father. *"He who has seen me has seen the Father,"* he said. Ask God to take you, his *teknon* (immature child), and make you into a *huios* (mature child). Ask God to empower you to prosper.

To be full of grace or God's empowering presence means that one can operate with divine help. We function using his strength, not our own. I don't mean by this that human effort or discipline will never need to be exerted; what I mean is that we become dependent on God. We learn to operate in partnership with the Almighty, not independent of him.

One of the things that prevent us from ruling and reigning in life is the absence of humility or its counterpart, the presence of pride. Most of us, if we are honest, will admit we are not strangers to pride. Pride or arrogance is an orientation that relies on self—self-centeredness, self-reliance, self, self, self. It often operates in conjunction with an independent spirit ("I can do it myself"). It is evident in our lack of prayer. Someone has wisely said that the amount of pride in our life is inversely proportional to the amount of prayer in our life.

Prayer is an expression of dependency on God. Humility recognizes that in ourselves, we can do nothing, and faith sees that in Christ, I can do all things. Prayer expresses these concepts to God in utter reliance upon him and releases the power and wisdom of God into the situation.

A second thing that can prevent us from ruling and reigning in life is the absence of submission (or a submissive spirit). This condition is often made more obvious by the presence of a controlling spirit or the need to control others or by the fear of being controlled. Controlling others through manipulation and personality is called witchcraft. It indicates a lack of trust in the Father. Its root is insecurity.

Many leaders and influential church people have controlled others rather than teach them and release them to the Spirit's control. This abuse, or the fear of abuse, has led many of us to a reticence in yielding to any form of leadership or authority (legitimate or not). Many of us think that church is a democracy because of the strong influence of our Western culture. We do not recognize or respond well to authority. Unfortunately, this reluctance to accept authority has hindered us in our progress in becoming more intimately acquainted with God's government.

There is hope for this dilemma because an accurate understanding of the kingdom of God will actually free us from the dominion of man's control. Understand that we enter the kingdom of God of our own free will. We volitionally surrender our will to the Lordship of Jesus. God does not violate our free will. Satan operates much differently. He enslaves. Learn to discern if the authority in your personal situation is forcing you to their point of view or encouraging you to make up your own mind according to the Word of God. Submission is never taken. It can only be given. Jesus was the perfect example of both humility and submission (Phil. 2:8).

A third hindrance to us ruling and reigning in life is deception. We are unsure of what he has promised us and what is really ours to claim. We don't really know the Word. Some of us are affected by a religious spirit and a spirit of poverty. We need to memorize the benefits of the cross. We need to know verses like Psalm 103:2-5: *"Bless the LORD, O my soul, and forget not all his benefits: Who forgiveth all thine iniquities; who healeth all thy diseases; Who redeemeth thy life from destruction; Who crowneth thee with lovingkindness and tender mercies; Who satisfieth thy mouth with good things; so that thy youth is renewed like the eagle's"* (KJV). We need to make a quality decision to believe what God says, not what our circumstances or senses tell us.

One of the things that many great men and women of God do is pray the Word. They take passages of scripture and consistently pray them until faith is realized. By studying and praying the Word, we can conquer deception and learn to overcome through Christ.

We rule and reign in life through recognizing his sovereignty, submitting to it, and by praying that his will be done on earth. We also rule and reign in life by seeing the promises, the blessings, and the benefits of our relationship with God and exercising faith in those promises. We pray the Word of God because it is the express will of God. We are partnered with Almightiness. Jesus has given us right-standing with God so that we can "ask to borrow the car" or utilize what is ours in the family of God. Jesus has also given us the empowering presence of the Holy Spirit, who enables us to do all things.

6

~ DISCIPLES OF THE KINGDOM ~

Letting Jesus be Lord

*"All authority in heaven and on earth has been given to me. Therefore
go and make disciples of all nations, baptizing them in the name of the
Father and of the Son and of the Holy Spirit, and teaching them to
obey everything I have commanded you."* (Matt. 28:18-20, NIV)

We have already looked at the great commission in chapter 3. To review:
"All authority in heaven and on earth has been given to me." This statement
is a declaration of the Lordship of Jesus Christ. He is, in fact, saying, I AM
God. He is stating his sovereignty. Many people forget this part of the
commission. This is a kingdom statement. The great commission is stated in
a kingdom context. Therefore go and make disciples of all nations: *Therefore*
alludes to the first statement. In other words, he is saying, because I am
sovereign, go and tell people in all ethnic groups. Make them my disciples.
Let them know me, for who I am, Lord. Make them subjects of my rule,
by baptizing them (immersing them in water) in the name of the Father
and of the Son and of the Holy Spirit and teaching them to obey.

What are we to teach new believers to obey? We are to teach everything
Jesus commanded us. It sounds like Jesus is under the impression that he
is in charge. He is saying, Go and teach people to obey my commands.

Apparently, we are supposed get them to come under God's government. *"And surely I am with you always, to the very end of the age,"* is the promise of his empowering presence.

A. Make Disciples

In this chapter, we study Jesus's statement *"Make disciples . . . by teaching them to obey everything I have commanded you."* A disciple is an apprentice—someone who is learning a trade or vocation. A disciple is a learner, and a disciple of Jesus is learning to let Jesus be Lord over his life. The evidence that I am letting Jesus be Lord is that I obey his commands. If I fail to learn his commands, I am not a good disciple. If I fail to obey his commands, I'm not a good disciple. If I fail to teach others, by my words and actions, to obey the Lord, I am not doing a good job of the commission Jesus gave, and I am not leading an exemplary life under his government.

How well are we doing at making disciples? Let me ask you to list the commands of Jesus that he was alluding to in Matthew 28:20. I dare say most of us would have a tough time doing that. It's just like the kingdom paradox. Those that represent the kingdom don't know what it is. Chances are you cannot list the commands by heart and are unsure of what they are. You are not alone. Most Christians in Western cultures do not know the commands of Jesus and whether or not those commands include only New Testament teachings or Old Testament such as the Ten Commandments as well.

I am not advocating a legalistic rule-based Christianity. Some of us have encountered legalistic flavours of Christian expression and are not excited about going back there. Kingdom theology is not asking us to return to legalistic bondage but to explore the reality of the Lordship of Jesus. Christianity is a relationship, not a rulebook. Our relationship is with a Ruler, the LORD of Lords. And how does one properly relate to a Lord? One responds to a Lord by giving obedience.

Kingdom theology recognizes justification by faith and impartation of grace as prerequisite to becoming a mature disciple. We don't obey rules to become right with God. We obey his rules because we are right with God. I could attempt to soften it up, but the reality I am trying to express is simply this: one cannot be under the rule of Christ without recognizing that Christ makes the rules. For too long, we have attempted to camp at God's mercy and forgiveness when all the while, he calls us to the higher walk of living in obedience. He calls us to grace, living life his way, in his strength. Making disciples has to, by Jesus's very definition, involve teaching commands and expecting obedience.

B. Nature of the New Covenant

Jesus is Lord, and he did tell us to teach disciples to obey his commands. Before we explore what those commands are, let us review the basis of the new covenant. God said that the new covenant would involve him putting his laws in our hearts and minds. Rather than write them on two tablets of stone, he would write them on the tablets of our hearts and the tablets of our minds.

> *For this is the covenant that I will make with the house of Israel after those days, saith the Lord; I will put my laws into their minds, and write them in their hearts: and I will be to them a God, and they shall be to me a people: And they shall not teach every man his neighbour, and every man his brother, saying, Know the Lord: for all shall know me, from the least to the greatest. For I will be merciful to their unrighteousness, and their sins and their iniquities will I remember no more.* (Heb. 8:10-12, KJV)

This is our covenant. It was made with the Jews in Jesus's day, and in Peter's day was opened to the Gentiles.

1.   I will put my laws into their mind, and write them in their hearts.

This is some of the clearest scripture regarding the new covenant. In this passage, it is clear that the new covenant involves the laws of God. Now the laws he speaks of here are not new laws but the existing laws. They are not the Rabbinical laws (with all the Jewish embellishments). They are not the Mosaic laws that deal with sacrifices for sins. Jesus did away with the need for sacrifices for sins, so all the Old Testament laws concerning cleansing and covering sin has been made redundant by a better sacrifice. God is speaking about the moral laws, or the laws that reveal his character and nature. (They also reveal what sin is—for sin is the transgression of the law.) He is speaking of the Ten Commandments.

2.   *I will be to them a God.*

So the first thing about the new covenant is that God will put his laws into our minds and hearts. Christianity is not, therefore, lawless. It cannot be, or we are outside of the covenant. Secondly, God says he will be God to us, and we will be his people. This not only points to a relationship but defines the nature of the relationship.

3.   *Know the Lord.*

The third thing about this covenant is perhaps the most important of all. All of those in this new covenant will know who God really is—LORD. What God is really after is for mankind to know him as he really is. God has had trouble over the centuries getting his people to really see him for who he is.

Discipleship is intended to acquaint us with the Lord and explain the relationship we have with the Almighty. This relationship is called the new covenant. Discipleship furthermore helps us to obey the commands that are written in our hearts—the law of God—so that we can walk with God in relationship.

C.   God has a Plan

Did you know that the Bible mentions twice that God is Love but it refers to God as Lord over seven thousand times? I have heard many messages about God being love but few about him being Lord. God has had problems communicating with us about this, or should I say, we have had problems understanding God?

**The Bible mentions twice that God is love,
but it refers to God as Lord over seven thousand times.**

God was very—I think you'd have to say—frustrated with his people in Isaiah Chapter 1. He said and I paraphrase verse 3, "The ox knows his master but my people do not know me." He had attempted many times to correct his people but was expressing his frustration that the punishment wasn't working. Read Isaiah chapter 1 and try to capture the main thought God is expressing, and I think you will see that it can summarized as, "There is a problem here. My people do not know I am Lord." In chapter 2, he gives a solution.

> *In the last days the mountain of the LORD's temple will be established as chief among the mountains; it will be raised above the hills, and all nations will stream to it. Many peoples will come and say, "Come, let us go up to the mountain of the LORD, to the house of the God of Jacob. He will teach us his ways, so that we may walk in his paths." The law will go out from Zion, the word of the LORD from Jerusalem.* (Isa. 2:2-3, NIV)

This prophetic portion of scripture outlines God's disciple-making operation in the last days. As we read this passage over carefully, we must bear in mind that it follows the declaration of God's frustration over the fact that his people fail to recognize who he is. His plan is to let people all over the globe know him for who he really is. We are going to look at this passage from Isaiah 2 very closely because it foretells the great commission.

"*In the last days*" means in the days from Roman times until now. This is explained in Daniel. Daniel also explains the meaning of mountain.

> *The head of the statue was made of pure gold, its chest and arms of silver, its belly and thighs of bronze, its legs of iron, its feet partly of iron and partly of baked clay. While you were watching, a rock*

was cut out, but not by human hands. It struck the statue on its feet of iron and clay and smashed them. Then the iron, the clay, the bronze, the silver and the gold were broken to pieces at the same time and became like chaff on a threshing floor in the summer. The wind swept them away without leaving a trace. But the rock that struck the statue became a huge mountain and filled the whole earth. (Dan. 2:32-35, NIV)

"In the time of those kings, the God of heaven will set up a kingdom that will never be destroyed, nor will it be left to another people. It will crush all those kingdoms and bring them to an end, but it will itself endure forever. This is the meaning of the vision of the rock cut out of a mountain, but not by human hands." (Dan. 2:44-45, NIV)

In the time of the Roman Empire, God will take a "Rock," which we know is Christ Jesus, and from that Rock make a mountain. The mountain, we have explained for us in verse 44, is a kingdom. The *"mountain of the Lord's temple"* is none other than the kingdom of God. The "temple," we know, is the church, or the redeemed people of God. The mountain or kingdom *"will be established as chief among the mountains; it will be raised above the hills,"* meaning that the kingdom will gain prominence over world governments. *"All nations will stream to it"* means that people from all ethnic groups will come into the kingdom.

Many peoples will come and say, *"Come, let us go up to the mountain of the LORD, to the house of the God of Jacob."* People from all nations will respond to the opportunity to enter the kingdom of God and will join the church—the house of God. *"He will teach us His ways."* The people entering the kingdom of God will be taught or discipled, so that they can walk the way Jesus walked (so that we may walk in his paths).

"The law will go out from Zion." Law means *torah*. Zion is the people of God. The people of God will go out with the *torah* (and the law will be a schoolmaster that brings people to Christ). *"The word of the LORD from Jerusalem"* refers to the prophetic proclamation of the Gospel. The good news of the kingdom, which must include the law, will be preached in all the world, and then the end will come.

The purpose of this whole operation is to bring to people all over the world an understanding of the fact that God is LORD. If you will confess with your mouth that Jesus is Lord, you will be saved. It is, of course, a description of the great commission.

The great commission that Jesus gave us is to go out and help people see Jesus for who he is—Lord. We are to die to our old life in water baptism and be instructed in our new life by learning and obeying his commands. Those commands will reveal the nature of God and include the Ten Commandments.

D.   What are the Commands of Christ?

Reading from the gospel of Matthew, we have about ten commands that all disciples must learn. Here is a list:

- Repent.
- Believe in him who was sent.
- Be baptized.
- Receive the Spirit.
- Love—This command includes all the Ten Commandments (Matt. 5:17). Love is the fulfilling of the Law. "Love your neighbour as yourself" is a summary. The Ten Commandments are more explicit (detailed).
- Pray (includes fasting).
- Forgive.
- Give (includes tithing and more).
- Go—heal the sick, raise the dead, preach the Gospel.
- Seek his kingdom (obey his Spirit).

Other commands include studying to show yourself approved, continuing in the apostle's doctrine, breaking of bread, and all the "one another" commands, like encourage one another daily, etc.

This list might seem like law, and "We are not under law but under grace." But what does this verse mean? It is possible that we read into this passage from Romans 6:14 and its companion Galatians 5:18 more than the Lord intended. We tend to interpret it as a relaxing of requirements. Paul himself said, *"To them that are under the law, as under the law, that I might gain them that are under the law; To them that are without law, as without law, (being not without law to God, but under the law to Christ,) that I might gain them that are without law"* (1 Cor. 9:20-21, KJV). Paul seemed to be without law and with law at the same time. He knew that the Mosaic Law, especially with all the Rabbinical adjuncts, could not justify him before God and had no power to make points with God. He did, however, recognize that we are under law to Christ.

E.   Grace and the Law

The church has a false understanding of what grace is, based on this verse: *"We are not under law but under grace."* This verse seems to say that grace is the *opposite* of law, where in reality grace and law are not opposites. They are both authored by God. If grace is the opposite of law and law means standards, rules, and obedience, then grace would mean a relaxation of the standards and rules, like when we give someone a grace period on a debt. They know it means we are cutting them slack or giving them extra time to pay. So we have read into the text a "relaxing of standards" that may not be there.

If we look at what Jesus said about the law in Matthew 5, we can see no such relaxation. In fact, Jesus said, *"Anyone who breaks one of the least of these commandments and teaches others to do the same will be called least in the kingdom of heaven, but whoever practices and teaches these commands will be called great in the kingdom of heaven"* (Matt. 5:19, NIV). As we read Matthew 5, we see Jesus adjusting the commands and, in most cases, raising the standard. For example, "Do not kill" becomes "Do not even hate or get angry."

Now it can be argued that Jesus was under Jewish law and fulfilled it. The implication being that we don't have to anymore. Jesus actually did do away with the need for the sacrifices for sins, the temple, and the Jewish priesthood. He did not abolish the moral law of God. A proper translation of the word *fulfill* is "made replete". It does not mean "satisfied all the requirements of". *Replete* means to fill up to the brim. Matthew

5:17 should be translated *"I have not come to abolish the Law or the Prophets but to make them replete"*.

Christians can confuse grace with gracious. *Gracious* means "disposed to show kindness and courtesy, mercy and compassion." God is gracious. It is his nature. We should be gracious as well. It is not gracious to be judgmental, rigid, or legalistic. But we carry "graciousness" too far if we allow it to overshadow the fact that as Lord, God can, and does, give us commands that, quite frankly, he expects us to obey. The reason God gives us grace is so that we can obey his government.

When someone says, "Yes, but we are not under law but under grace," they often mean we can't be expected to obey the Word of God, especially the Old Testament. Some verses in Titus seem to contradict this idea. *"For the grace of God that brings salvation has appeared to all men. It teaches us to say 'No' to ungodliness and worldly passions, and to live self-controlled, upright and godly lives in this present age"* (Titus 2:11-12, NIV). Grace teaches us to say "No!" to what the law taught us was wrong. Graces teaches us to live godly lives, and that implies standards. Jesus was full of grace, and we don't see the Father cutting him slack.

Another verse we often hear quoted is "By grace we are saved . . . not by works." *Grace* is connoted to mean mercy and forgiveness. *Works* connotes human effort at keeping standards. Most times, when we quote Ephesians 2:8-9, we forget to quote Ephesians 2:10: *"For by grace you have been saved through faith, and that not of yourselves; it is the gift of God, not of works, lest anyone should boast. For we are His workmanship, created in Christ Jesus for good works, which God prepared beforehand that we should walk in them"* (NKJV). There is another way to look at this passage.

Works is from a Greek word meaning "energy, effort, or work." We have read it this way—we are saved by God's forgiveness rather than by our own effort, but maybe Paul could be saying you are saved by God's energy, not your own energy. For by divine influence and power you have been saved. It wasn't your own influence and power but what was given to you by God that saved you. So you can't boast. We are all his handiwork and were created by God to do good works (works authored or authorized by God), which God previously prepared for us to walk in (to obey). The same grace that saved you empowers you to work. I don't see God cutting us slack here, nor do I see any cutting of slack in the life of Jesus or in the teaching of Jesus, especially in Matthew 5:17-22.

> *Think not that I am come to destroy the law, or the prophets: I am not come to destroy, but to fulfill. For verily I say unto you, Till heaven and earth pass, one jot or one tittle shall in no wise pass from the law, till all be fulfilled. Whosoever therefore shall break one of these least commandments, and shall teach men so, he shall be called the least in the kingdom of heaven: but whosoever shall do and teach them, the same shall be called great in the kingdom of heaven. For I say unto you, That except your righteousness shall exceed the righteousness of the scribes and Pharisees, ye shall in no case enter into the kingdom of heaven. Ye have heard that it was said by them of old time, Thou shalt not kill; and whosoever shall kill shall be in danger of the judgment: But I say unto you . . . "* (KJV)

(Read the remainder of the chapter and you will see Jesus tightened up and raised the standards, rather than cutting them slack.)

We don't need God to lower the standards. The new covenant isn't about lower standards. It's about getting help from God to do his will. We need his divine influence—his indwelling presence—to empower us to rule and reign in life. If we are to operate under his government, then we need more power, more strength, more joy—in other words, more of God. This help and strength, this blessing from God is part of grace. Lay hands on your head and ask God for more grace. Humbly ask for his blessing of the abundance of grace.

As a disciple of Christ, I am to obey all that he has commanded, not in order to become accepted by him, but because I am already his child. I have a covenant with God, and in that covenant are laws. These laws will free me from sin's control and save my soul. God has already saved my spirit and given me access to his grace so that I can say no to sin and yes to God. As we, by the grace of God, do what Jesus tells us to do, we will enter into the freedom and maturity of the sons of God. We will rule in life. Jesus wants others to know this glorious truth, so he has commissioned us to tell others about his kingdom. The next chapter explains the Gospel of the kingdom.

7

~ THE GOSPEL OF THE KINGDOM ~

The Law is a Schoolmaster that Leads us to Christ

What purpose then does the law serve? . . . Is the law then against the promises of God? Certainly not! . . . Therefore the law was our tutor [or schoolmaster] to bring us to Christ, that we might be justified by faith." (Gal. 3:19; 3:21; 3:24, NKJV)

Because of the fullness of Him we all received one blessing after another, because the law through Moses was given; grace and truth through Jesus Christ became. (John 1:16-17, Greek transliteration)

In the second chapter, we defined the kingdom of God as the government of God, or the rule of Christ. The kingdom is found in the Holy Spirit and centered in serving him. Now we let this functional definition work through into our understanding in other areas. Obviously, the Gospel, or good news of the kingdom, must have something to do with government.

I don't know anyone who is looking for more government in their lives. I can think of some who would like less government. I am not suggesting that we hit the streets proclaiming the good news of more government. What we need is not more government, but a change to good government. What people need, like it or not, is to see that their lives are governed by sin. They think they are free, but they are enslaved by an evil master, sin. The Gospel of the kingdom offers us a good master, who has the power to overthrow sin and free us from its control. The Gospel of the kingdom doesn't offer freedom from control, but rather offers to replace sin's control with the Spirit's control. Once under the Spirit's control, you will not be controlled by fear or sin.

The Modern Gospel of Life Enhancement

The Gospel message we are familiar with offers a salvation package that is tailor-made for our consumerism mentality. Come to Jesus. He loves you. He died for you. He offers eternal life. We hear a plea to make a decision. We say a simple prayer, and *poof!* We are saved. There is only one problem. Ninety-six percent of converts fall away in less than a year. That holds true for crusades, church evangelism, event evangelism, para-church evangelism, etc. Ask the evangelistic organizations and the charismatic and non-charismatic denominations—this statistic is true here in the West, across the board.

We repudiated the hellfire preaching of the 1800s and early 1900s and preached love and mercy. We have been effective in convincing the public that God is love to the point that most people in the West think they will automatically go to heaven when they die. Here in Canada, 90 percent of people polled claim they believe in God. Ninety percent of the "believers" think they will go to heaven. That means 81 percent of Canadians think they are going to heaven. Only about 5 percent are born again. Not too many fear hell anymore. And because people think God is all goodness and no severity, they don't fear him either.

Since there is little or no fear of God and no fear of hell in our society, we aim our message at life enhancement rather than preparing for the afterlife. Jesus will heal you. Jesus will make your life better. Jesus will give you peace. Jesus will give you joy. People answer the evangelistic appeal but fall away when they don't experience peace and joy. Some preachers mention sin and the need to repent but, unfortunately, the message has difficulty penetrating because people today don't really know what sinners are. Rather than understand the biblical meaning of *sinner*—as anyone who has transgressed God's law—they see a sinner as a truly immoral, evil person, which they obviously are not.

People today are not convinced that they are lost. Everything is relative. When we tell them Jesus died for their sins, it's like telling them we have the cure for a disease they don't know they have. If someone told me that I could be cured of polio, I wouldn't care because I don't have polio. We need to help people see their sickness before they will be interested in the cure. The modern Gospel concentrates on giving the cure. It begins with what Jesus did for sinners. What we need to do is back up and help people see that they are, in fact, sinners, convince them of it, and then tell the convinced to repent and warn them to flee the wrath to come. To do this, we use the law—the law was our tutor (or schoolmaster) *to bring us to Christ, that we might be justified by faith*. We need to clear up the common misconception that "everyone who isn't a mass murderer automatically goes to heaven."

The Gospel of the Kingdom

The Gospel of the kingdom is the good news about freedom from sin's control and the wonderful opportunity to be under God's control instead. So we must communicate the nature of God and the nature of sin before we give them the great news of Jesus's death and resurrection. The Gospel can be outlined as follows:

1. God's position
2. Man's condition
3. God's provision
4. Man's decision

The modern gospel starts with God's provision, which is the third point in the outline. The first two points provide the necessary foundation for wanting to receive God's provision. We don't have to preach hellfire. In fact, a look at the Gospels reveals that Jesus spoke about hell while teaching his disciples, not while doing evangelism.

The pattern for preaching the Gospel is right in front of our noses. It is so simple we missed it. Before Jesus came to preach, God sent a forerunner—John the Baptist. Under his ministry, people repented of their sins. They knew what to repent of (sins) through the preaching of the law. The purpose of the law is to reveal sin. *"Through the law we become conscious of sin"* (Rom. 3:20, NIV). The law convicts us of sin and convinces us we are sinners. The law gives the Spirit something to convict us with.

> **Indeed I would not have known what sin was**
> **except through the law.**

> *What shall we say, then? Is the law sin? Certainly not! Indeed I would not have known what sin was except through the law. For I would not have known what coveting really was if the law had not said, "Do not covet." (Rom. 7:7, NIV)*

John preached the law of Moses. This preaching prepared sinners to hear the grace and truth that Jesus brought *"because the law through Moses was given; grace and truth through Jesus Christ became"* (John 1:16-17, Greek translation). God gives law to the proud and grace to the humble. Jesus would be hard with people who wanted to be self-justified. A perfect example is the rich young ruler.

> *A certain ruler asked him, "Good teacher, what must I do to inherit eternal life?" "Why do you call me good?" Jesus answered. "No one is good—except God alone. You know the commandments: 'Do not commit adultery, do not murder, do not steal, do not give false testimony, honour your father and mother.'" "All these I have kept since I was a boy," he said. When Jesus heard this, he said to him, "You still lack one thing. Sell everything you have and give to the poor, and you will have treasure in heaven. Then come, follow me."* (Luke 18:18-22, NIV)

The young man asked, *"What must I do to receive eternal life?"* Jesus pointed him straight to the Ten Commandments (the encapsulation of the law). The ruler asserted that he had kept them since his youth. Jesus refrained from pointing out the obvious. (All have sinned and fallen short—Rom. 3:23.) There was some major pride and self-delusion in this ruler's mind.

So rather than confront the man's ignorance, Jesus simply suggested he give his money to the poor. In saying that, Jesus was referring to the first commandment: "Thou shalt have no other gods before me." Mammon (money) is a false god and is widely accepted and worshiped in most every society. Jesus didn't argue with the man's false claim of never breaking God's commands, He tested the man's faith using the first commandment. Jesus gave law to the proud.

Jesus gave grace to the woman caught in the act of adultery, who was about to be stoned. She already knew she was a sinner. She was humbled. Jesus said, *"I don't condemn thee. Go and sin no more."* God gives law to the proud, grace to the humble.

The Gospel of the kingdom begins where the sinner is. If he knows he needs God and is ready to repent, then start with God's provision. If he feels he's okay without God, plant the seeds of God's law to prepare his heart for conviction. The law is a schoolmaster that brings us to Christ. The Ten Commandments make an excellent evangelistic tract.

Now we will fill out the four points:

1. God's position
2. Man's condition
3. God's provision
4. Man's decision with a bit of detail

On the next page is an outline, followed by notes on subsequent pages.

Outline of the Gospel of the Kingdom

God's Position

- Eternal, intelligent, creative, powerful, all-knowing
- Sovereign LORD
- Morally perfect, honest, just, pure, holy
- Good, does not change, has a plan and a will for us (Ten Commandments)

- Sin is transgression of his will and has consequences
- Hates sin and judges sin
- Loves us

Man's Condition

- Created in the image of God to obey God and have fellowship with God
- Has a free will to choose whether to obey or disobey God, has chosen to disobey (sin)
- Cannot avoid the consequences of God's judgment of sin
- Has a goodness that falls short of God's standard
- Is completely lost
- Will be found guilty of sin and will go to a godless eternity

God's Provision

- Blood of the lamb
- Riches of Egypt
- Moses (leadership)
- Angel
- Pillar of smoke and fire (guidance and protection)
- Separation of Red Sea
- Law (government)

Man's Decision

- Repentance
- Faith
- Water baptism
- Holy Spirit baptism
- Teaching
- Fellowship
- Works of faith

I. God's Position

God's Attributes:

- He is omnipotent—infinitely powerful, supreme, unlimited in power
- Invincible (victorious), awesome, terrifying
- Imaginative and creative
- Intelligent beyond description or our comprehension
- A Spirit and a person distinct from creation but holding it together
- Invisible unless he chooses to manifest himself, omnipresent (in all places)
- Omniscient (all knowing—past, present and future)
- Eternal (without beginning or end)
- Immortal (lives forever)
- Immutable (not changing)

God's Attitudes:

- Is morally perfect
- Absolutely honest
- Completely fair (just)
- Absolutely pure
- Totally loyal
- Holy
- Good—kind, merciful, forgiving

He exists. "I am that I am." *"He that comes to God must believe that He is."*

He is Lord. That is his name, not his title. It is his nature. That God is Lord is mentioned over seven thousand times in the Bible. The Lord our God is One.

He has a will. As Lord, he has a plan and purpose for his creation. He has a will that he wants done. His moral will for mankind is summarized in the Ten Commandments. (His moral will give us insight into His character.) God expects us to submit to his will, not ignore or reject it. When we act contrary to this will, we sin and suffer the consequences.

The Ten Commandments summarized (See Exod. 20 and Deut. 5):

- You will have no other gods beside me.
- You will not make idols or any graven image.
- You will not use the name of God in vain.
- You will keep the Sabbath holy.
- You will honour your parents.
- You will not murder.
- You will not commit adultery.
- You will not steal.
- You will not bear false witness.
- You will not covet what others have.

He does not change. The God of the New Testament is the exact same God as the God of the Old Testament.

He hates sin. Sin is harmful to us. Sin is evil. Sin is anything against God. God gave his people the law to define or reveal sin. Failure to keep the law is transgression. The law did not create sin. Sin reigned from Adam to Moses. The law cannot remove sin. Like a mirror, it merely points out what looks bad but cannot correct it.

He judges sin. He compares others to himself. He doesn't mark on the curve. He is not supertolerant. He is just. He does not overlook or ignore sin. He is perfect, and that is his standard. He is good, and because he is good he will judge all sin. God demonstrated painfully clearly in the Old Testament that he does, and will, judge sin. Look at these biblical "news headlines:"

- Couple Banished from Garden of Eden
- Millions Annihilated in Universal Flood
- Alternative Sexual Orientation Advocates Vaporized in Twin City Disaster
- Egyptian Army Drowned in Red Sea Phenomena
- Ten Reconnaissance Agents Executed for Spreading Negative Report
- Generation Dies in the Wilderness
- Seven-Nation Genocide

He is Love. God loves us. His love is *agape*—a commitment to do right for another regardless of emotion. His love is not sentimental indulgence or mere affection. His love will not excuse or ignore sin. He loves us despite the fact we are sinners, not because we are lovable, but because it is his very nature to love. True love will not overlook sin but will expose sin and destroy it. Those he loves, he disciplines.

II. Man's Condition

Man

- has limited power,
- is vulnerable,
- is somewhat creative and imaginative,
- has limited intelligence,
- has a spirit and a soul that live in a body,
- is a created being made from mud and returns to mud after death,
- is visible,
- is limited to one place at a time,
- knows a few things (sees through a glass darkly),
- is not eternal (had a beginning),
- is mortal (it is appointed unto man once to die), life span eighty years,
- is mutable (can change)

Man

- is immoral to some degree,
- selectively honest, lies,
- unfair, biased, bribable, corruptible,
- impure (in words, thoughts, and actions),
- varies in loyalty, self-centered,
- unholy, sinful,
- good to a point (his goodness falls short of God's standard, so much so, that God considers man's goodness as filthy rags—literally the menstrual cloths of a prostitute)

Man was created

- by God for God's pleasure,
- in the image of God,
- to have fellowship with God,
- to obey God,
- to have dominion of the earth (while recognizing God's sovereignty over the earth, but man failed to obey that sovereignty and fell under the control of Satan)

Man was given free will (to choose to obey or disobey God—major importance).

- He has chosen to disobey God.
- He transgressed God's will (moral law) and must face the consequences.
- The consequences are that many innocent suffer.

Man has sinned. He transgressed the law of God. Because he sinned,

- He is separated from the life of God.
- He will die.
- He is abiding under the wrath of God.

Man will be judged by God.

- He will face judgment (without exception, without excuse, without a doubt).
- He will not be marked on a scale but against God's standard.
- He will be found guilty.
- He will go after judgment to an endless existence in a Godless place of torment.

Man cannot save himself.

- He cannot acquit himself by his own goodness, religion, or works.
- He cannot earn salvation, merit salvation, or purchase salvation.
- He is completely lost.

III. God's Provision

Because God is love, and because he has a purpose for mankind, he has a desire to redeem man from sin. God did not create mankind to have them all lost for eternity. God has provided a solution to man's dilemma. This solution gives man the opportunity to exercise his free will to choose to accept or reject it. God's solution was to pay for the sins of mankind himself. This solution came at a tremendous cost to God. The following is adapted from Philippians 2 and hopefully will give the reader a small insight into the price God paid for our salvation.

Jesus—the immortal, invincible, omnipotent God of all creation, whose very words had so much creative power that things literally burst into existence at his mere mention of them—this Jesus laid aside his royalty, majesty, and unlimited ability and humbled himself to become nothing (of no reputation). The One who contains in himself the whole universe, funneled himself into a tiny package.

The Lord of lords, whom all creation will bow their knee to and to whom all should give their devotion, worship, and service, became a servant. The eternal Holy God fashioned himself into a human body, into the form of the unholy ones, who rejected and refused his Lordship. In becoming human, he chose to be born into a poor family, not a royal family or a rich family. He faced the ridicule and social stigma of being a child conceived out of wedlock. He further humbled himself and became obedient to his parents and to the law of God. He was totally submitted to the will of God. He never sinned.

The sinless one, the absolutely innocent one, the keeper of all the law, willingly allowed himself to be beaten and executed as a criminal. He took upon himself all the sins of mankind and was cut off from the face of the Father. He was obedient to a horribly gruesome death, death on the cross. Then, taunted by unholy demons, he descended into a godless pit of despair, the place of torment, to finalize the arrangement for our release. This solution cost God more than we can imagine.

God extends his grace (his unmerited favour towards sinners that enables them to do what he requires in his strength) to sinners. Grace is offered free simply because we haven't the remotest chance of paying the tiniest fraction of the cost. The gift God offers us is absolutely priceless. (Free for us, but costly to God.)

God sent his only son, Jesus Christ, to be obedient, to be executed, and to go to hell on our behalf. He "that knew no sin" became sin for us and was judged and sentenced. Jesus shed his own innocent blood in the same manner as the Passover lamb's blood was shed. Jesus and the Father both suffered unimaginable hurt and anguish to free us from sin. God has made his provision so that anyone, anywhere, can choose to accept it. God, the Son, has provided his own blood as a solution to wash away sin.

**The solution to man's condition is offered
free, simply because we haven't the remotest
chance of paying the tiniest fraction of the cost.**

Jesus provided for us more than just pardon from sin. We already looked over the brief sketch of the benefits of the cross in an earlier chapter. In the chart below, which parallels the experience of the Israelites as they escaped Egypt, we look at some of the provision of God in salvation.

1.	Blood of Passover lamb	Blood of Jesus, cleansing from sin
2.	Riches of Egypt	Wealth, talent
3.	Moses as leadership	Human leadership
4.	Angel as leadership	Divine leadership
5.	Pillar of fire/smoke	Holy Spirit as protector and guide
6.	Separation by water	Water baptism
7.	Water (bitter to sweet, from the rock)	Refreshment, living water
8.	Food (quail and manna)	Nourishment, bread of life
9.	Government (law)	Holy Spirit as divine government

When a sinner decides to become a Christian, he must understand that he is committing to becoming a disciple. Those of us who are mature believers are told by our Lord to make disciples of all nations, baptizing them, and teaching them to obey all that he commanded. Therefore, the sinner must, first of all, repent and turn to God in faith. He must understand and accept God's provision of the blood as the one and only solution for his sin.

The innocent blood of the lamb speaks of the blood of Jesus that cleanses away our sin and saves us from death. This aspect of God's free gift of salvation is the most prominent and best known. It is the provision of the blood that pays the price that I cannot pay. But the blood is not all that God provided. We have been provided with natural gifts and talents that came out of Egypt with us. You might have been a good piano player before knowing Christ. Now you might be able to offer your talent in the building of God's tabernacle.

God has provided the child of God with both human and divine leadership. To be made into a disciple requires that you have a disciple maker, who will teach or apprentice the young Christian. Jesus gave the church apostles, prophets, and other inspired teachers.

A new convert must become aware of the Holy Spirit. The Holy Spirit has been active in their lives bringing them to Jesus Christ. He has protected them and will continue to protect them. He has led them and will continue to lead them. He will help them learn the scriptures and empower them to be witnesses for Christ.

The Red Sea separated the Jews from Pharaoh. This represents God's provision called water baptism that cuts us off from the world and its hold on us. Water baptism allows us to die to what once controlled us and rise in newness of life under the dominion of God. It is an essential step in escaping from sin.

God provides us with water and food in a spiritual as well as a physical sense. The Word of God is bread to us, and it washes and refreshes us. We need to be in the Word daily.

Finally, new believers must be taught that being a Christian means obeying God. Obedience to God is not a means to salvation but certainly the product of it. True believers have a new nature—they want to obey God. It was Adam's disobedience that started sin in the first place. As a restored man, we now must respond properly to God's sovereignty—in other words, we obey God.

As we become disciples, God gives us a new heart in which are written his laws. He puts his law in our heart by the Holy Spirit. The Holy Spirit, if allowed to control us, will empower us to do all that God desires. We therefore need to understand and receive the baptism of the Holy Spirit.

We cannot effectively operate in the kingdom of God without the Spirit. The Holy Spirit is the governor in the government of God.

Jesus Christ came to save us from sin. It must be communicated that being saved is more than fire insurance (safe from hell). Jesus promises an abundant life, but he also promises trials, tribulations, and persecutions. We are saved from sin by the grace of God. That grace will also enable us to overcome sin in our daily walk. Grace will not excuse or overlook sin. Grace will teach us to be godly. True salvation is not about escaping hell, although with it comes an assurance and peace that we are safe from hell. True salvation is about dying to sin and living for God.

IV. Man's Decision:

After hearing and understanding the Gospel, a man must make a faith response in order to receive salvation. Salvation is not automatic but must be personally taken hold of by each individual. "What must I do to be saved?" is the response we hope to get, although we may also get crying (contrition is good) or any number of questions or responses. At the heart of a proper response is **a commitment to the Lord Jesus**. If a person wants to believe in Jesus but refuses to be discipled or water baptized, then one doubts the genuineness of their decision. Ideally, you will want to see the sinner respond and complete the following.

1. **Repentance**—A mental recognition that I have done wrong in the eyes of God. A verbal confession of sins (specific) addressed to the Father. This is why it is so important to teach the Ten Commandments to the unsaved so that they will know what to repent of. A conviction to right what can be righted, i.e., to reconcile past broken relationships or to make restitution for past wrongs. A determination to turn away from those sins and any sinful lifestyle. For example, someone living with their girlfriend will have to move out of that arrangement to avoid future fornication.

2. **Faith**—A belief and a trust in the words of the Gospel message. An understanding and acceptance of Jesus Christ as Lord. A verbal confession that Jesus is Lord. A willingness to act in obedience to Jesus's commands.

3. **Water baptism**—Immersion of a believer in water for their separation from sin and the world's reach. A physical act that has spiritual impact. Death to the dominion of self and Satan and a new life in submission to the LORD. Some teaching will be required, especially for those who were "baptized" as babies. (Infant baptism overrides the child's free will and is not acceptable to God as a proper baptism.)

4. **Baptism in the Holy Spirit**—Scripture teaches us to believe in Jesus and to receive the Spirit. Each new convert needs to experience the infilling of the Holy Spirit. One should expect a manifestation such as speaking in tongues or even prophesy as being normal and appropriate. Normally, some teaching is required.

These four steps are necessary for one to come under God's government. The next three are also vital for the ongoing health of the newborn.

5. **Commitment to being taught**—Though not normally listed as a requirement in order to be a disciple, it is definitely implied. A new convert needs to embrace some kind of discipline that includes Bible reading, prayer, and personal instruction from a mature saint. The early believers continued in the apostle's doctrine and prayer.

6. **Commitment to fellowship**—Part of our new commitment to Jesus Christ includes a commitment to his body, the other believers. It is vital to the life of a new Christian to have some involvement in a local church.

7. **Commitment to works (of faith)**—Having been saved by the works of Jesus (not our own works), we now enter into a lifestyle of allowing him to work in and through us. Believing is not just a mental exercise but a foundation for doing things that God wants done. One of the things God wants to do through us is to witness to others about Jesus and share the Gospel. He wants to use our hands in helping others, our feet in going to others, our lips in praying for others, our mouths in speaking to others, our faith in laying on hands and praying for the sick or giving a word of wisdom to someone. He wants us to use our resources to help others, equip others, and support others in the work of the kingdom.

People will respond to the real gospel. The Word of God promises it. We need to cast off the flimsy modern gospel and embrace and preach the message that the apostles preached. *"Then the angel showed me the river of the water of life, as clear as crystal, flowing from the throne of God"* (Rev. 22:1, NIV). We need to rid the river of God of the pollution of man's gospel and get back to a message that aligns people with the throne of God.

> *In the last days the mountain [kingdom] of the LORD's temple will be established as chief among the mountains; it will be raised above the hills, and all nations will stream to it. Many peoples [unconverted] will come and say, "Come, let us go up to the mountain of the LORD, to the house of the God of Jacob. He will teach us his ways, so that we may walk in his paths." The law will go out from Zion, the word of the LORD from Jerusalem. He will judge between the nations and will settle disputes for many peoples.* (Isa. 2:2-4, NIV)

There is going to be a great harvest in these last days. I have written this book to help you understand the kingdom of God so that you can preach more effectively and prepare new converts to go up to the "mountain of the Lord." As they get a proper foundation laid in their life, they will turn the world upside down with the Gospel of the Lord Jesus Christ.

~ GLOSSARY ~

Grace—Divine influence, undeserved or unmerited favour. Very often grace is understood to be unmerited but without the appropriate understanding of what favour is. Favour is the noun and is more important that the adjective. We have so under emphasized *favour* and over emphasized *unmerited* that in our minds grace equates to mercy. Grace is not mercy it is power. The empowering presence of God's Spirit enables us to do the impossible. God's strength and energy given to the humble (dependent on God), which saves them, heals them, and enables them to do the will of God, including turning from sin and working miracles.

Justification—When God says, "Not guilty!" It is a process that turns one from being a sinner under the wrath of God into someone accepted and adopted by God. The penalty for sin is paid in full by the blood of Jesus. When we first believe in Jesus and confess him as Lord, we are by faith justified before God, just as if we'd never sinned. It is a gift from God. There is a complete change of legal status. This change is so comprehensive and dynamic it is called "becoming a new creature" or, in effect, a new species.

Kingdom of God—The realm of God; that which God rules over. A territory or people ruled by a king, in this case the King of kings. The kingdom of God is essentially the government or rule of Christ. (Christ in us, the hope of glory, is the Holy Spirit.) *Kingdom theology* is teaching that emphasizes the centrality of the Lordship of Jesus Christ. It points to the Spirit-controlled life. This teaching reveals the true nature of God

UNDERSTANDING THE KINGDOM OF GOD

(that he is sovereign) and the true nature of man (that he needs redemption and, once redeemed, can rule with Christ). The kingdom of God is the central theme of the whole Bible.

Law—Can mean principle, as in "The law of the Spirit of life has set me free from the law of death." The word *law* most often refers to the *Torah*, which means "teaching or instruction." In other words, "law" means the teachings of Moses, and in particular, the moral law of God as summarized in the Ten Commandments. If you think about it, the Ten Commandments are the only words God gave his people that he actually wrote in his own handwriting. They are a transcript of the nature of God and are unchanging and eternal. The law is good, holy, and of great usefulness and benefit to the Christian. Faith upholds the law, and love fulfills the law. It cannot justify one from sin. It simply reveals sin. It reveals our need for Jesus.

New birth—The process of initially coming under new government. It is an act of God, whereby he plants his incorruptible seed into our spirits, and we are made alive spiritually. It is an act of man, whereby he recognizes the reality of God, accepts or believes the Lordship of Jesus by faith, and confesses with his mouth that "Jesus is Lord." He turns from the control of sin and enters into the government or kingdom of God. (See *Justification.*)

Sanctification—The process of maturing, whereby the carnal or flesh nature of the born again person (Christian) is taken over by the rule of Christ. Some call it the salvation of the soul. Justification is a rather quick process in which our spirit is made alive. We are born again or adopted and become children of God (*teknon*). Sanctification is a rather long process, where that life in our spirit influences and permeates our soul. Our actions, behaviours, thoughts, and motives are transformed to become reflective of divine influence. We, in effect, become like Jesus, a mature Son of God (*huios*).

~ SUGGESTED READING ~

1. Pawson, David. *Truth to Tell*. London: Hodder & Soughton. 1993.
2. Comfort, Ray. *Hell's Best Kept Secret*. CA, USA: Whitaker House, 1989.